TO STACEY,

MAKE LIFE

FUN—

IMPROVISE!

BEST,

Improve with Improv!
The Art of "Yes..."

The Improv EDGE

How the art of improv can
boost your confidence, enrich
your life and fast-track you to
a more energized and motivated
presence!

Joe Hammer

Published by Forerunner Publishing, Scottsdale, Arizona
ISBN: 978-09968047-1-4

Bound and printed and in The United States of America

Cover design by Joe Hammer, That Small Business Guy
www.ThatSmallBusinessGuy.com
Edited by Michele Berner.

To buy additional copies of this book, visit the author's website at www.TheImprovEdgeBook.com or www.Amazon.com

For more information on Joe Hammer's speaking, improv and business training services, please contact him via his official web sites:

www.YourImprovCoach.com
www.ThatSmallBusinessGuy.com
www.TheOutcasters.com

Here's to the crazy ones. The misfits. The rebels. The troublemakers. The round pegs in the square holes. The ones who see things differently.

They're not fond of rules. And they have no respect for the status quo. You can quote them, disagree with them, glorify or vilify them.

About the only thing you can't do is ignore them. Because they change things. They push the human race forward.

And while some may see them as the crazy ones, we see genius. Because the people who are crazy enough to think they can change the world, are the ones who do.

– Steve Jobs

Dedication

Robin Williams
1951 - 2014

There will never be another improv magician like Robin Williams. His comedic physicality, flowing jokes and dazzling impressions set the bar for the art improv at the highest level. His stage antics were grueling, but he never failed to deliver...
...and his audiences always desired more.

Robin's incomparable talent could make serious moments immeasurably hilarious or mindless instances reflect deeply-rooted meaningfulness.

He has inspired me as well as thousands of other improv practitioners to dig deep for "real-world funny" through the art of improvisation. He is sadly missed.

Rest in Peace Robin.

Note from Author: I would normally include a photo of Robin with this dedication, however he has legally restricted commercial use of his images until 2039, 25 years after his death. Although many continue to display his photo, I chose to honor his wishes and not include it here.

The *Robin Williams Trust* has passed the rights to his name and likeness to *The Windfall Foundation,* a philanthropic organization that raises money for many charities, including *Doctors Without Borders, The Pediatric AIDS Association* and *Make-A-Wish Foundation,* as well as California charities, *Project Open Hand, University of California at San Francisco* and *San Francisco General Hospital Pediatrics.* I would urge you to support those organizations as a tribute to Robin's gifts to improvisation.

You're only given a little spark of madness. You mustn't lose it.

– Robin Williams

The Stuff Inside...

Introduction 1

A Note to the Reader 9

Chapter #1:
What is "Improv?" 13

Chapter #2:
The History of Improv 19

Chapter #3:
The Improv State of Mind 23

Chapter #4:
Energizing Our Weakened Creativity Muscles 27

Chapter #5:
The Science of Funny – Our Brains During Improv............... 33

Chapter #6:
You Have Permission to Imagine! 41

Chapter #7:
Mindfulness IS Improv.. 45

Chapter #8:
Quieting That Pesky Inner Critic... 51

Chapter #9:
Failing Without Failure... 61

Chapter #10:
Creativity – Intelligence Having Fun! 67

Chapter #11:
From Blah to Ta-Da! 79

Chapter #12:
The Often-Ignored Roles and Objectives 83

Chapter #13:
The Lost Art of Active Listening... 87

Chapter #14:
Hey, Make Me an Offer I Can't Excuse 95

Chapter #15:
Yes, I Accept Your Offer! 101

Chapter #16:
Don't Be a Block Head 111

Chapter #17:
Huh, You're Questioning Me? 117

Chapter #18:
Mistakes as Gifts 123

Chapter #19:
Specificity 135

Chapter #20:
The Secret 55% Communication Tool 141

Chapter #21:
The Power of Object Work 149

Chapter #22:
Conscious Consideration 155

Chapter #23:
From the Stage to the Boardroom 161

Chapter #24:
Team Building 165

Chapter #25:
Some Final Words from the Author 171

Chapter #26:
Improv in the Movies 183

Chapter #27:
Let the Games Begin 187

About the Author 209

Introduction

During the summer months in the 90s, my buddy and I would often head to New York City on the weekends. It was a great way for a couple of small town Ohio boys to increase our blood pressure, test our rudeness and sharpen our bad attitudes. From checking out the latest threads at the garment district on 42nd or negotiating a gold chain based on weight at the diamond district at 47th, the city always delivered a great time, and if you were street smart, you could score some great deals on just about anything.

> As an aside, when it came to comedy in the Big Apple, *Dangerfield's* club was my favorite. I once met Rodney there. His sweaty and nervous stage demeanor was just the opposite of the humble and warm-hearted man he was. Amazing how a small, intimate club could have so much energy and fun times, especially when he took the stage. He definitely got my respect!

One weekend, we were thinking about going to the China Club for a drink, but we saw a sign on 22nd, in front of what used to be a strip club, saying something about an "Upright Citizen's Brigade." We didn't know what that was, but after walking up to the window and reading the bill, we discovered it was the new home of an improv comedy group by that name.

I had an interest in this unique form of comedy, as I had done some improv training in Pittsburgh to complement my stand-up magic-comedy work at that time. I talked my buddy into foregoing the over-priced drinks at the China Club, so we could check out the UCB show.

We showed up, and I have to say it was a pretty dumpy place. However, once the players energetically took to the stage, I totally forgot about the cobwebs, musty odor and clutter. We were mesmerized by their show called "ASSSSCATT," where a simple audience suggestion prompted an improvised monologue from one of the cast members, which then inspired a series of improvised scenes.

Brilliant stuff.

The Upright Citizen's Brigade's work was based on "The Harold," a type of long-form improvisation conceived by actor, writer and teacher, Del Close. Del was the "go to" coach for many comedians and comic actors, including John Belushi, Gilda Radner, Bill Murray, Mike Myers and Chris Farley. He later left NYC and went on to perform and direct at The Second City in Chicago.

The show was fabulous, and I wanted to learn more about it. I picked up some information on their workshops as we were flying home the next day. From that point on, I made it a point to visit the theater, study their shows and participate in their training every time I visited the city... many times the reason I visited the city. I was always amazed at the level of talent in the minds of those wacky people.

Since that experience decades ago, I have continued to study, participate and train in improvisation. Further, I routinely implement its time-proven principles into my speaking and entertainment programs. Improv has become a viable tool in my everyday life, and I enjoy teaching it as much as I appreciate performing it.

I am writing this during a historic "pandemic" time. I'm on lockdown with my chihuahuas, and my workload has lightened up a bit, so I felt there was no better time to author a dissertation on the many benefits of an art form I truly adore... so here it is, *The Improv Edge!* In it, you will discover pearls of wisdom from the spontaneously created, unplanned and unscripted world of improvisation.

More importantly, you'll also discover how to implement the valuable principles behind the art of improv into your life. You may be thinking, *"C'mon Joe, I don't want to be funny."* That's okay, you don't have to. But after understanding the ideologies of improv, you'll discover it's not just about being funny, it's about reacting, being focused and fully present in the moment, and all at a very high level.

Improvisation will provide you with higher levels of creativity, innovation, communication, teamwork and leadership. You'll learn how to think on your feet and how to react and adapt to the unexpected things that life will deliver to you. Improv is about being present in the moment and being comfortable with the things you're most afraid of.

And you'll do it all while you're learning how to become a better person!

Oh, and if you change your mind and decide to be funny, join me for an improv class. I can't promise it'll be more fun than Disneyland, but you'll feel just as good when class is over.

To your Improv-abilities,

Joe Hammer
September 19th, 2020
Scottsdale, Arizona

PS - You may think 27 chapters is a lot to consume but rest assured, I made them all appetizing and bite-size delicious!

PPS - A special thanks to all my improv peeps in Los Angeles, New York City, Phoenix and Scottsdale who provided wisdom about their experiences with improv; they had my back... Yes, and... *they're awesome too!*

Improv is the most important group work since they built the pyramids.

– Bill Murray

Improve with Improv!
The Art of "Yes..."

The Improv
EDGE

How the art of improv can
boost your confidence, enrich
your life and fast-track you to
a more energized and motivated
presence!

Joe Hammer

*Improvisation is the practice
of unplanned observation,
unbridled acceptance and
compelling reaction.*

Joe Hammer

Note to the Reader

Congrats on selecting *The Improv Edge*. Unlike most personal development books, *The Improv Edge* will not offer you "rah-rah" techniques to change your life, but instead, afford you unconventional, yet highly effective and flexible tools to become not only enormously more effective in your communications but also get more fun out of life!

Some people believe improv is too difficult and something they could never do, when, in fact, it is actually a very common human experience. We improvise every single day of our lives! During a conversation with a friend, do you know the words that will come out of your mouth before uttering them?

Whether on stage in front of a live audience, giving a presentation, managing staff or working with a development team at your office, the tools of improvisation are formidable instruments, ready to be used in everyday situations occurring in your life.

That's what I call the improv "Edge."

New students come to improv for a variety of reasons. Many have been "dared" to try it, while others have been sent by their company or organization. Some have come with friends just to give it a try. New students sometimes find their initial efforts not all that productive, many times awkward and sometimes not funny, but as soon as they embrace the rules of improv, the magic begins to happen. They become hooked and embrace expanding their talent and knowledge of the art! After participating in the practice of improvisation, most everyone finds it can make pretty impressive changes in their life.

In an improv scene, something needs to happen. A story needs to be told. Almost all improv scenes require a relevant beginning, a smidge of background information, a twist (something different that happens in the scene), an understanding of how it all connects, and a reasonable ending.

And you need to create it all with information you receive in a moment's notice.

Sound scary? It's really not. Improv training teaches you how to agree and move forward ("Yes, and..."), supporting of others ("Got your back!"), adapting quickly to change, speaking with conviction, being decisive, and actively listening. We're going to talk about all of that and more in *The Improv Edge*.

As you know, the best things in life are those exciting moments where you let yourself go and have fun. You already have everything you need to do that. Many of us attempt to plan our days, covering as many details as possible, but the magic happens when we let go and give ourselves space and permission to play.

Improv is an art form, where you are invited not to take yourself so seriously. You don't need techniques or "punchlines" to be funny. Nor do you need theatrical training, styles or humorous concepts in order to be good. As improvisers, we are out of our minds... that is, we spend time out of our analytical mind, allowing our creative mind free rein. In doing so, we are more fluid and joyfully allow our natural ridiculousness to come out and play!

Improv can be scary and rewarding at the same time; however, there are a lot of wonderful lessons that can be learned from this engaging art form. It's not only about exercising a playful mind but also about active listening, open collaborating, and creativity; skills at the heart of every human being. Students learn how to work together to create relationships, environments, situations, and conflicts – and all without the comfort of a script!

As improvisers, we are out of our minds

To genuinely grasp the fundamentals of improv, it's important that we recognize the value of spontaneity in our daily interactions. Sadly, we've become accustomed in doing routine things day in and day out. We greet people the same way. We take the same route to work. We utter the same response when we're asked how our day is going. With improv, it all starts with stepping out of our familiarity mindset - our comfort zone - and reacting in a different way. We're going to talk about how to do that and more, so fasten your seat belt, my friend!

We are all improvising our way through life. Life is improvisation. I encourage you to be present and become more aware of the process of "making it all up" as we go! Now, gently roll your sleeves up, grab a cup of coffee, fist bump your neighbor and let's get to work exercising the power of *The Improv Edge!*

Your Take-Aways:

- *Tools of improvisation can be used in everyday situations occurring in your life.*

- *Improv invites you not to take yourself so seriously.*

- *You don't need techniques or "punchlines" to be funny.*

Chapter 1

What is Improv?

Some unassuming chairs are positioned on an otherwise blank stage. That visual can be chilling to the new improv student; however, the veteran improv practitioner sees it as an opportunity -- an opportunity to add content to the empty stage, opening up to the possibilities around them.

They are ready to utilize everything from nothing in a scene *whose story is yet to be discovered!*

When many hear the word "improv" (shortened form of the word, Improvisation), they often think of conventional "skit" shows at their local comedy club. These most often start with two or more players on stage, and the audience is asked for a single suggestion – a relationship, scene or circumstance.

From there, the improv players create a complete show, knowing nothing about where they will be going. They generate characters, a story, and moments of meaningful engagement... as well as unexpected twists and turns. They take the audience on a unique journey to places yet to be discovered by everyone involved.

Improv is the wonderful art of creating something out of nothing.

Wikipedia describes Improvisation as *"the activity of making or doing something not planned beforehand, using whatever can be found. Improvisation in the performing arts is a very spontaneous performance without specific or scripted preparation. The skills of improvisation can apply to many different faculties, across all artistic, scientific, physical, cognitive, academic, and non-academic disciplines."*

It further states, *"Improvisation also exists outside the arts. Improvisation in engineering is to solve a problem with the tools and materials immediately at hand."*

To improvise is to expand and heighten the discoveries in the moment.

Human beings are natural improvisers. We improvise most every day of our life. We've instinctively learned how to roll with the punches and handle life's challenges with whatever tools we have at the time the challenge is put before us. If you've ever put together a dinner, arranged a birthday party or fixed a broken vase, you've improvised! How many times have you used a knife edge or key to turn a screw? And if it weren't for *Duct Tape* or *Super Glue,* many of us would miserably fail at improvising a fix for an unexpected broken trinket! Heck, even parenting is improvised, as nothing truly prepares us for it!

When improvisers hit the stage, they simply make things up on the spot. Unscripted. Instantaneous.

Improv is like a high wire act without a net. However, there's a lot more to it than simple entertaining. The techniques improv players use on stage can be robustly harnessed and used as tools to assist us in everyday challenges–from family to relationships, workplace to colleagues, there are many opportunities to flex your improv muscles and experience life and career in a more spirited way!

Yes, improv can renovate our lives for the better!

Individuals who have studied improvisation tend to feel more relaxed in both their lives and careers, as their personal life is a lot more fun. They see disappointments and life's occasional botches as opportunities. Like their work on stage, they embrace whatever is handed to them as gifts, ready for a positive reaction and resolution.

Life has no script; we are all born improvisers.

Anyone can learn and engage the principles of improv. People who train in improv seek engagement with their fellow players by consistently trying something new. Most find these skills assist them in more effectively leading and collaborating with their fellow workers off the improv stage.

Many therapists have studied and utilized principles of improv in therapeutic modalities in assisting clients with a number of mental challenges. I have personally used it in my clinical hypnotherapy practice. From general well-being to anxiety to academic performance, we become more spontaneous in responding to our client's needs by using the principles of improv.

> *Life has no script; we are all born improvisers*

It's also a powerful treatment for boosting creativity. A study by researchers at the University of Michigan and Stony Brook University found that just 20 minutes of improv experience causes people to feel comfortable and more tolerant of uncertainty.

The results of a study titled *Improv Experience* promotes divergent thinking, uncertainty tolerance, and affective well-being, published by Elsevier, indicated that improvisational theater training could improve divergent thinking. Further, it found new findings that improv can boost positive effects and increase uncertainty tolerance relative to other social interactions. [1]

[1] https://bit.ly/3onMQTL

It's been said that "planning is essential, but plans are useless." Well, there's only one plan in improv, and that's the plan to have fun!

Outside of the few times in our lives where we methodically sweat over delivering a rehearsed speech, every one of our daily conversations is improvised!

Your Take-Aways:

- *Life has no script; we are all born improvisers.*

- *To improvise is to expand and heighten the discoveries in the moment.*

- *Improv allows you to be more relaxed in your life and career.*

- *Improv allows you to embrace whatever is handed to you as gifts, ready for a positive reaction and resolution.*

I took stand-up classes and performed for six years prior to taking improv. I was resistant to the idea. I mean, stepping on-stage with no idea of what's coming? That seemed frightening!

In my view, the real connection between stand-up and improv relates to the building of confidence. Even though they both take place on stage, the difference is that most stand-up is tightly scripted. Even my "spontaneous lines" were heavily rehearsed. Improv, however, is "in-the-moment."

In my improv experience, scene partners are friends, sharing the performance on stage. All they ask is that you do the same for them. In stand-up, you're on your own. If your set goes South, there's no one else to blame. In improv, you're never alone!

That's the thing with improv, you don't have time to endlessly ponder multiple options; you must act instinctually as well as instantly. After leaving the stage, I often ask myself, "Where did that line or action come from?" I guess it was always there; it just needed a gentle nudge and removal of the filter that used to hold it back.

Improv classes are not like a CPA course, where everybody's quiet and repressed. Classmates become good friends. It's the only class where you're an even bigger success if you mess up badly. Can nuclear engineers say the same thing?

Joe Frank
Scottsdale, Arizona

Chapter 2

The History of Improv

Improvisation's history dates back as early as *Atellan Farce* in 300 BC in Ancient Rome. It later was active in the 1500s in *Europe as Commedia dell'Arte,* where groups of traveling performers created shows with improvised dialog. Theatrical improvisation, as we know it today became mainstream in the 20th century, mainly through the efforts of theater academics, acting coach and educator Viola Spolin (1906-1994). Viola creatively assembled theater games as a method of training improvisational acting. Others offering similar training were her son, Paul Sills (1927 - 2008), as well as Del Close, Joan Littlewood, Clive Barker, Keith Johnstone, Jerzy Grotowski and Augusto Boal, to name a few.

Viola Spolin

These improvised games were commonly used as warm-up exercises for actors before a rehearsal or performance, as well as in the development of improvisational theatre. Further, it was also an imaginative means to rehearse dramatic material, assisting in overcoming anxiety by simulating scenes that would be fear-inducing in "real" life.

Viola Spolin's son Paul popularized improvisational theater, as he was the founding director of the *Compass Players* - which led to the formation of the *Second City Theater* in Chicago, the very first improvisational theater company in the United States.

Paul used his mother's techniques in the training and direction of the company, creating satirical improvisational theater about current social and political issues. He held workshops for Second City actors as well as the general public. Paul Sills and the success of Second City were largely responsible for the popularization of improvisational theater, which became a comedy form called "Improv."

Improv players quickly embraced the art, discovering the value of their training by uncovering their natural talents, intuition and creative behaviors. By working with other players, improv comedy came naturally – without conventional jokes and punchlines.

The Second City Theater opened in December 1959 and has since become one of the most influential comedy theaters in the world. Many actors, writers and directors came out of Second City and had formative experiences performing and being trained there. These include highly successful and notable graduates like Bill Murray, Gilda Radner, John Candy, John

Belushi, Dan Aykroyd, Del Close, Eugene Levy, Catherine O'Hara, Nia Vardalos, Mike Myers, Steve Carell, Tina Fey, and Amy Poehler, as well as many, many others.

Improvisation was seldom demonstrated on television until the master improviser Robin Williams came onto the scene in the situation comedy, *Mork & Mindy*. He was allotted specific sections in each episode, where he was permitted free rein to perform as he desired, using his highly-developed comedic improv skills.

Improv theaters have since sprung up all over the world, teaching improvisation comedy to all walks of life. Shows like *Thank God You're Here, Kwik Witz* and *Whose Line Is It Anyway?* soon skyrocketed the popularity of improvisation comedy on televisions all over the world. Stars like Drew Carey, Ryan Stiles, Colin Mochrie, Brad Sherwood and Wayne Brady soon became synonymous with hilarious televised improv games.

Contemporary improv troupes continue to demonstrate their talents all over the globe, usually working in small theaters and comedy clubs, performing impromptu scenes based on ideas and suggestions from the audience. Through weekly improv training, players continually perfect their skills in emotional responsiveness to very imaginative situations.

Working in the higher education industry as a Bursar in New York City, there are times when I need to speak in front of students and colleagues. My fear of public speaking had hindered that. In a professional environment, it's not always easy to have an answer readily available to a question or a concern that may arise.

Taking improv classes has allowed me to feel more comfortable when the attention is on me. Improv warmup games have assisted me in building skills that help in providing quicker responses. The 'Yes, and...' rule has been a valuable skill in customer service, as well as in dealing with coworkers on issues that often arise.

Improv has given me an outlet to step outside my comfort zone and acquire new skills that I can apply in everyday life, both personal and at work. Laughter is always the best medicine. With improv you laugh at yourself often, then move on to another moment. When you can incorporate that into an uncomfortable situation, you can alleviate a great amount of the pressure and accept who you are instead of judging yourself.

Erin Angarola
Bursar
New York City, New York

Chapter 3

The Improv State of Mind

Spontaneity. Confidence. Creativity. Trust. Acceptance. Commitment. Listening. Character. Support. Teamwork.

Do any of these sound like traits you may like to put to work in your life, relationship or career?

Then you must say YES to improv!

Improv doesn't rely on pristine acting skills or how "naturally funny" you may be. An improv state of mind is an optimal one. Improvisation isn't about comedy; it's about actively listening, reacting, and being focused – all while being present in the moment at a very high level. In a performance setting, it means listening to what a fellow player says, accepting what was said without rejection, then building upon it. In business, it means accepting any and all ideas brought to the table, then adding to them.

Using techniques and rules of improv, we can rehearse and refine our communication skills and enjoy a more jubilant version of ourselves to our families, jobs and daily routines.

Improvisation reflects creativity, innovation, communication, teamwork and leadership. It teaches you how to think on your feet and how to react and quickly adapt to unexpected events and circumstances you didn't plan for.

The emotional side of decisions and organizational dynamics is of utmost importance to successful interactions. Improv training will amplify your comfort with objective facts as well as providing you with balanced emotion and expressiveness.

Improvisation reflects creativity, innovation, communication, teamwork and leadership

As humans, we are social creatures, and improv inspires us to truthfully see, hear and value others, all of which strengthens relationships while encouraging risk-taking and innovation.

Whether selling your idea to a loved one, supervisor, co-worker or audience members during a presentation, improv training will enhance your skills. After engaging in improv and returning to the office, you soon realize how many small things you thought were important truly didn't matter!

Improv thinking is akin to that of "flow state." In his book, *Flow: The Psychology of Optimal Experience,* author Dr. Mihaly Csikszentmihalyi describes flow as *"the optimal psy-*

chological state when one is engrossed in activity." He indicates that during flow states, time can be distorted, and individuals can lose their reflective self-consciousness.

Many refer to this state as being "in the zone." This is the playground of improvisers when they put their inhibitions and self-doubt aside and boldly focus on their fellow players and the scene at hand.

Okay, are you ready to join the improv community? We'd love to have you!

Your Take-Aways:

- *Improv doesn't rely on acting skills or how "funny" you may be.*

- *We are social creatures, and improv inspires us to see, hear and value others.*

- *Improv teaches you how to think on your feet, react and quickly adapt to unexpected things.*

As an Asian-American, improv was quite different from anything I grew up with. I had never taken any acting or theater classes, but decided to try improv as a way of improving my public speaking and shyness in front of groups. Do to the crippling anxiety I had, I could feel the tension throughout my body; it was immensely difficult for me when I first started.

After a few classes, I was quickly able to improve my listening and communication skills. I learned exercises that focused on repetition, mirroring, and building on other's ideas while contributing my own. I learned to embrace positivity and collaboration with my scene partners on stage, something that was unheard of before my improv training.

I grew to love improv and its ability to bring out my own unique voice, which had somehow been hidden within me for so long. I feel extremely lucky that I've found improv; it's now a hobby I'm passionate about!

Steve Ling
Insurance Professional, Co-Founder of Improv NOW
New York City, New York

Chapter 4

Energizing Our Weakened Creativity Muscles

There are hundreds of improv games. Each one has a different angle in exercising and re-energizing creative muscles that have become atrophied from our historical recordings and day-to-day living. We've become a victim of limiting and self-destructive patterns and unconscious scripts placed in our minds by others ... and we've grown to believe they define us.

Our subconscious minds hold onto everything from our past.

I refer to our subconscious programming as the *Unconscious Authority,* as it directs us without awareness from our conscious minds. To further explain this phenomenon, here is an excerpt from my book, *The Unconscious Authority: How to Break Through Your Mind's Barriers, Unleash Your Dormant Wisdom and Banish Limitations in Your Life, Relationships or Career* [1]:

[1] *The Unconscious Authority*
The Forerunner Publishing Company, ISBN # 978-0996804707

The Master Recording Device

... every event, sensation and experience of your life has been masterfully recorded in your mind. The depth, strength and accuracy of these recordings are unlike those from any man-made recording device in history. Not only are the details of these events masterfully recorded, but the intensity of the event, sensation or experience you were exposed to is also part of this historic recording. This recording device works 24 hours a day, seven days a week. It's a work-a-holic.

The *Unconscious Authority* carries out duties, missions, operations and assignments housed in our subconscious minds, our virtual "storage center" for all types of commands, instructions and guidelines since childhood.

Parents, family members, siblings, teachers, counselors and others of perceived authority have influenced us during our childhood in many ways. From being called a "bad" boy or girl to being referenced as "careless," "stupid," "ditsy," "lazy" or "sloppy," many times, these statements are uttered to "teach us a lesson;" however, the long-term results are often just the opposite.

Most of us have experienced these remarks in some form or another during our impressionable childhood years. Please understand, I acknowledge our loved ones meant well when uttering these statements. Unfortunately, most well-meaning parents were unaware of the negative impact their words could have on our growth and future.

Oh, and if you grew up around inspiring statements like being called a "princess," or that you were a "special" kid, you'll soon discover how those statements could actually have negative consequences in your adult life as well.

Our outward life is a manifestation of what we are within. The Unconscious Authority got its training instructions early in our lives.

Authority Figures Curse

Parents, grandparents, friends, relatives, teachers, members of the clergy, counselors, siblings, nannies, babysitters; they all have influenced us in some way. And they did so when our mind was an open door, unshielded from their unfavorable words. Along with this influence from others came their belief system, attitudes, perceptions, childhood experiences and historic programming. In other words, these people dished out their opinion, guidance or direction before we were intellectually developed to accept or even understand it!

Their stuff soon became our stuff.

As adults, we are still being programmed by authority figures; however, the players have changed. From your boss or supervisor to the nightly news anchor, your doctor to your investment advisor, these perceived "authority" figures are still active in our lives.

When a doctor advises a patient what is necessary to eliminate or better manage their illness, the patient carries out the instructions, conceding the doctor's recommendation is an accepted truth. However, another person with the same illness visits a faith healer who merely touches the patient's head, and they soon recover without the need for medications. The common denominator in both circumstances is belief. Studies related to prescribed placebos have proven that the belief in the medication outperforms the actual chemical benefit.

Our subconscious minds hold a powerful grip on our past programming, and we silently follow along to its navigation system. We've become accustomed to following the rules, color inside the lines and seek to find that one "right" answer. Through this flawed training, we have stifled our creativity, challenged to take risks and have become a zombie to life's circumstances.

Here's a little exercise that you'll find fascinating:

Connect all of the dots, using only four lines, and without lifting your pencil from the page. Again, connect all of the dots, using only four lines without lifting your pencil from the page:

Well, how did you do? Found it difficult, right? Well, head to page 211 for the answer (as well as the "lesson" behind it).

You're probably wondering what all this "mind stuff" has to do with improv, right? The bottom line is this... *We have been coached to be safe, overly cautious and less inclined to expose ourselves to risk.* It has become our nature to avoid doing anything outside of our comfort zone for fear of looking silly, uneducated or experiencing failure.

Because criticism, complaints and avoiding mistakes all tend to be prominent in our world, spontaneity and humor take a back seat to what we perceive to be the more stable and meaningful solutions. We rely on easy and sometimes comfortable choices, holding on to what we perceive to be the "right" answer. In doing so, it eventually becomes cozier to say no, and we put our playful side in the backseat.

Improv breaks us free of this conditioning and opens us up to expose our creative selves. It allows us to lighten up, look around and see things in a more joyous light. It provides an alternative to the controlling ways many of us have learned. It urges us to say "yes" and be helpful instead of argumentative in life's challenges and situations.

Once you ignite improv into your life, you'll break free of lame, pattern-like thinking and get your creativity rolling again. You'll soon see the beauty in coloring outside of the lines.

Why? *Because they are your crayons!* Are you ready?

Your Take-Aways:

- *We've become a victim of the limiting and self-destructive patterns and unconscious scripts placed in our minds by others ... and we've grown to believe they define us.*

- *We're taught to follows the rules, color "inside the lines" and look for the one "right" answer.*

- *We rely on comfortable choices and seek the "one" right answer.*

- *We put our playful side in the backseat.*

- *Improv opens us up to expose our creative selves!*

Chapter 5

The Science of Funny... Our Brains During Improv

Through active listening and focused attention, improvisation training strengthens our capacity to cope with uncertainty, manage anxiety and boost our creative thinking. Being open to our fellow players requires a nose-to-the-grindstone effort, risk and engagement. This makes us more adaptable to piloting the increasingly complicated world we live in.

Improv is actually a creative experience that nourishes our brains! A 2017 study published in the *Journal of Mental Health* looked at improv as a therapeutic intervention. It found meaningful improvement in symptoms of anxiety, depression, and reduction of perfectionism (which is a significant source of stress). That's great news, right?

Couple this with the laughter and social bonding produced by improv's imaginative interaction, and we have the foundation for a creative, socially rewarding experience. We'll enjoy the benefits of positive behavior therapy without the discomfort and costs of a shrink!

Improv creates "just enough" discomfort to trigger our minds to react outside of our conventional left-brain analytical processes. As a result, we are blessed with strength and greater adaptability when we're faced with a stressful life event or situation. Further, we discover better receptivity to ideas from others.

You don't need any controlled substance to experience the mind-bending euphoria that improv brings to your consciousness. While experiencing the thrill of concocting witty moments and fascinating scenes, we exude tiny, drug-like neurotransmitters... and all happening without our conscious awareness or slipping cash to a thug on the street corner.

The practice of improv delivers a blissful quartet of neurotransmitters, molecules responsible for your happiness and delight. They are *Endorphins, Dopamine, Serotonin and Oxytocin.*

In our everyday life, it's often a challenge in getting these critters released into our system, however improvisation will come to the rescue and assist in putting them to work for you!

Endorphins

The endorphins' job is to reduce our pain and boost our pleasure. No more, no less. Endorphins act on the opiate receptors in our brains. In doing so, they give us that ever-sought-after feeling of well-being.

Endorphins are released in response to pain or stress. They

are also released during more positive experiences, like eating chocolate cake, enjoying a calming yoga class, or having sex. Endorphins bring joy, and we always strive for more of it. The laughs of improv training will cause your brain to release more of them in every class.

Yeah, I guess you could say that your improv class instructor will become your drug dealer of choice.

Dopamine

When we achieve an objective or goal, we get a nice little shot of dopamine. We feel great after checking off items from our to-do list or surpass our last bowling score. It's our brain's way of rewarding us for getting things accomplished.

Dopamine is gradually released. The closer you get to reaching your target, the more is discharged. That's why we get more and more excited as we are getting close to achieving our goal, score or objective.

For those of us who are more obsessive about doing something, the effect of dopamine assists us in getting more focused. You may have heard this process referred to as the "flow" state or being in the "zone."

Improv games and scenes are always putting forth pintsized objectives you need to grasp onto. Solving the "problem" of moving a scene forward becomes the focus of the games. When it is solved, all the players feel great – and that's the result of the dopamine infusion! Nobody else is required to obtain dopamine and endorphin neurotransmitters; you can obtain them all by yourself. However, your fellow players make their delivery a lot easier!

Serotonin

Serotonin is a chemical that's obtained through our status. They're the little buggers that deliver us those mesmerizing feelings of pride and accomplishment... like the energetic round of applause we get after landing a fabulous improv scene. And once we get it, we feel more confident... (and cool, of course).

And, as your improv coach, I too get a secondary shot of serotonin! It's a win-win!

Oxytocin

Oxytocin provides us with a feeling of safety against danger. When we are among the people we love and trust, oxytocin is present and can be further triggered through a simple handshake or a warm hug. Thoughtful improvisers always strive to make their partner look good. These are a professional entertainer's *acts of kindness*. Acts of kindness, whether on stage or off, discharge oxytocin. Improv students routinely provide each other with a well-deserved dose of oxytocin when they exchange "I got your back" confirmations in the green room before hitting the stage.

These neurotransmitters powerfully assist us in a more contributive lifestyle. When you offer your energy of time, talents or gifts to make another person's life better, not only will you enrich their life, but you will also feel better yourself! Further, the more of it you have flowing through your body, the more you will desire to share it through assisting others.

Improv assists in overcoming your own fears by discovering how to help others overcome theirs. Combining this with the influx of oxytocin, you will boost your immune system, increase your problem-solving abilities, enhance your creativity and actually deter addictions!

And if that's not enough science for you... let's take a closer look at your brain and what happens during the practice of improvisation.

The Prefrontal Cortex

Improv really boosts our brain functionality. *The Prefrontal Cortex* is located in the frontal lobe of our brain and assists in planning complex cognitive behavior, personality expression, decision making and moderating social behaviors. The basic activity of this brain region is the arrangement of thoughts and actions in accordance with our internal goals. The psychological term for this is *executive function.*

According to Wikipedia's explanation of this process, it's *"our abilities to differentiate among conflicting thoughts, deter-*

mine good and bad, better and best, same and different, future consequences of current activities, working toward a defined goal, prediction of outcomes, expectation based on actions, and social 'control' (the ability to suppress urges that, if not suppressed, could lead to socially unacceptable outcomes)."

The downside of the prefrontal cortex is that it actually interferes with the generation of our creative ideas. Charles Limb of the University of California, San Francisco, conducted a brain scan of musical improvisers. Using an MRI (the technology that produces detailed images of the organs and tissues in the body), the results concluded that this particular area of the brain is "turned down" or "deactivated" during improvisation!

Further, this area of the brain - when involved in the assessment of an idea - is reduced, allowing the emergence of new ideas, similar to what takes place during daydreaming or meditation.

That's all good news for us improvisers!

Another area of the brain affected by improv practices is the *Default Mode Network* (DMN). It's best known for being active when a person is not focused on the outside world. During DMN, the brain is at a wakeful rest, such as that during daydreaming, mind-wandering, when we are thinking about others, thinking about ourselves, remembering the past or planning for the future.

During the practice of improv, there is strong evidence that DMN is deactivated. This is because we become more involved in discovering the exterior world and less involved with managing our inner world... that is, our judgement, self-awareness and preoccupation with other things.

Rick Hansen of UC-Berkeley's Greater Good Center says, *"... Neurons that fire together, wire together. Mental states become neural traits. Day after day, your mind is building your brain."*

Heavy stuff, but totally in alignment with the power of improv's ability to assist us in truly "changing" our minds!

And finally, there's **Neuroplasticity**...

Once we begin taking advantage of nature's drug addiction, we will soon have much more power in shaping our reality. This is due to our brain's amazing morphing power, known as *neuroplasticity*. Neuroplasticity is the brain's ability to change its physical structure and function through thought, emotion and activity. It's a huge scientific truth discovered over the last decade. Unlike what was previously thought, the adult brain isn't hard-wired, but flexible and able to take on new dimensions in growth!

Because nothing in your brain is truly hard-wired, neuroplasticity can replace unhealthy and undesired behaviors patterns in your own life with ones better aligned with your desires. To do so, you must consistently practice the new habit, and over time, your brain will eventually respond by making permanent changes and fortify the new behavior!

Our brain has the ability to change from the day we're born until the day we die. During that time, neuroplasticity is happening every minute of the day, whether you have an awareness of it or not. That known, why would we not use it consciously for our good rather than allowing it to unconsciously work against us?

Okay kids, science class is over. Hopefully, you have picked up what I put down...

Your Take-Aways:

- *Improv training strengthens our capacity to cope with uncertainty, manage anxiety and boost our creative thinking.*

- *Our brains deliver us cool drugs that help us in not only improv, but in life as well.*

- *Parts of our brains are turned down or deactivated during improv, allowing us greater creativity.*

- *Banish undesired habits by understanding Neuroplasticity.*

Chapter 6

You Have Permission to Imagine!

The word improvisation often provokes thoughts of stage fright and fear of the unknown. The seasoned improvisor, however, sees the potential of opportunities and adventures into the unknown. They see a chance to engage with others, play and make stuff up! The greatest scenes emerge when two people allow themselves to be vulnerable.

My experience with improv has demonstrated that people of all ages and backgrounds have chosen to become motivated, to step out of the box of life's predictability and embrace the thought of spontaneous conversation... creating something out of nothing! Doing so requires us to release our wonderful imagination! Part of that process is quick thinking, building from other's ideas and playing to the top of our intellect.

"It is the silence between the notes that makes the music;
it is the space between the bars that cages the tiger."
— Zen saying

Have commitment to your imagination. It's more than merely

making the audience laugh; they must care about your character and become engaged in the imaginative reality you've created.

Our wonderful imagination allows us to disconnect ourselves from the fear of mistakes, and the principles of improv permit us to be comfortable with making slipups.

Many times, we fail to initiate the creative imagination center of our mind. In an improv scene, we often face potential danger. After all, who knows what's going to come out of our mouths, right? How will it be judged by my fellow players? The audience? How will we know if it's right or wrong?

These destructive thought patterns can disconnect us from our imagination and water down our energetic and creative ideas.

We must embrace what is perceived to be dangerous!

Many of us have become accustomed to surveying a scene, situation or circumstance, and observe as much information as possible before taking action. This is the case with the classic "over-thinker." Do you know some? If not, it may be you!

Social anxiety holds many of us back from reaching our full potential. We are afraid of what others may think. With improv, you don't have the time to get stuck in your head; you have to keep the scene moving. If you wait for the "perfect" thing to say at the "perfect" time, nothing will ever happen.

The improv muscle, once exercised and toned, will assist you in taking fast, bold and decisive actions in your life.

The best way to change almost anything in life is to continually lean into it. Train yourself to relax through exposure to whatever it is that's perceived to be the challenge. In doing so, you release your imagination to do its job.

When we're new to improv, many times we talk too much. We unconsciously do this to preserve and keep the scene breathing, but by doing so, it usually ends up in a noisy blur of nothingness. If you cut your partner off, you will always miss a critical part of their message, which will not only frustrate them but may also destroy an amazing scene.

The improv muscle, once exercised and toned, will assist you in taking fast, bold and decisive actions in your life

In improv, there's a fine line between responding quickly and pausing to pull the best from your imagination. There's no distinction between responding quickly and responding applicably. Pausing creates tension, which draws the audience in. Comedic epiphanies happen in real-time and without your need to "be funny."

That's where imagination rules. The same is true in life; take a pause, but don't overthink it.

Turn your imagination loose. Improv will make you feel relaxed, happy, fulfilled, satisfied, proud, gratified, honored, rewarded, confident, loved and oddly enough, protected!

Your Take-Aways:

- *See and embrace the potential of opportunities and adventures into the unknown.*

- *Have commitment to your imagination.*

- *If you wait for the "perfect" thing to say at the "perfect" time, nothing will ever happen.*

- *Expose yourself to whatever it is that's perceived to be a challenge in your life.*

Chapter 7

Mindfulness is Improv

Jon Kabat-Zinn, a leader in the field of mindfulness, defines it as *"paying attention in a particular way; on purpose, in the present moment and non-judgmentally."*

Sounds like improv, right?

The policies of mindfulness are fully aligned with the fascinating world of improv. Both mindfulness and improv are incredibly powerful tools, ready to be put to work in today's demanding world. They allow us to accept and embrace an emotion or situation - the way it shows up - without the desire to control it.

Being mindful is something we improvisers are trained to do. And the best part? Through their laughter and applause, the audience actually rewards us for it!

The more mindful we can be in our improv work, the more mindful we can be in our career, communications, relationships and life in general. By aiming to be in the present, rather than thinking about all of the other things in our head, we are better listeners. We can respond more authentically in the moment. We are relaxed under pressure and confident in our direction!

Both mindfulness and improv provide us:

- *The capacity to actively listen and respond*

- *The knowingness of being more present in the moment*

- *The skill to welcome and embrace uncertainty*

- *The competence to receive and demonstrate kindness*

- *The cultivation of generosity*

- *The ability to start anywhere!*

How does something like mindfulness, often referenced as "quieting the mind," possibly align to the loud antics of improv stage performers? Well, it's what's *behind* all that banter wherein the harmonies lie.

Let's briefly explore the commonalities between the two...

In mindfulness, we are taught to leave our troubles behind. We teach the same process in improv. If the day's stresses and challenges are stuck in your mind, you are distracted from focus and not present. Your creativity in the scene suffers.

Improvisors have to pay astute attention to what is going on with their partners at all times. It is only through focus and awareness that they can understand what's happening. Only then are they able to add effective information and support to the scene. Using words, body language and object work, they can respond appropriately.

Improvisers are active listeners (detailed in Chapter 13). Not only do they *hear* their fellow players but *observe* them as well. They must be present. If they are thinking about what happened five minutes earlier or what direction the scene should take in the future, they are no longer in the present moment.

Just as there is no "starting point" for mindfulness, starting points can exist almost anywhere in improv. By recognizing and embracing uncertainty, we suspend judgement–creativity and spontaneity rule supreme. If an in-the-moment idea arrives (and it always does), time isn't needed to refine or evaluate it. We do not have a script to follow. We just exercise the wonderful liberty of being present in the moment!

Improv and mindfulness both allow generosity to be shared. Improv players have each other's back and exercise generosity by making everyone look fabulous in their supportive roles.

If you think about it, active listening and positively responding are two of the most generous things you can offer to another person! We are so busy doing, doing, doing that we forget just to "be" and deeply experience present moments.

You can become a master of mindfulness through improv. You can slow down those burdensome random thoughts that take up precious space in your brain. Improv will quickly have you seeing how magnificent present moments really are!

Later, I'll be covering the primary rule of improv, the "Yes, and..." rule. This rule advises that we must accept what is given to us from our fellow improviser in a scene and build from it. Just as you honor them with your uninhibited agreement, they are also obligated and honored to offer the same to you.

Let's see how mindfulness plays into this. Take a look at the questions below. How would people who are important and significant in your life respond to them? How would you respond to them if they were asked of you?

> *Do you see me?*

> *Do you hear me?*

> *Do you care about me?*

> *Do I matter to you?*

The word "yes" is the deciding factor in answering these questions. Everyone wants validation; it's a common desire in humanity. We all want to know we matter. That being said, wouldn't it be obligatory for us to pass this validation along to others?

People desire and need to be inspired. When they are inspired, they see what they can achieve or become. Be the one who inspires them. Whether a fellow performer, supervisor, team member or life partner, inspiration begins with active listening. We must be present in the moment and acknowledge. When you acknowledge a person, you demonstrate a recognition of their value and importance.

There's no better training in all of this than through improv.

How many times have you been in a conversation with someone and quickly discovered their mind is obviously in another place? Unfortunately, passive listening is all the rage today. People just nod their heads while eagerly awaiting their turn to speak. They think it's okay to look at their cell phone during a conversation.

Whether on stage, in the boardroom or having a conversation with a friend or loved one, we must be fully present.

If I start an improv scene by saying, *"Hey Charlie, I had a flat tire this morning,"* and he responds with, *"Hey, I was thinking maybe we should go to the casino later,"* he was not only failing to listen but obviously had an alternative plan as to where he desired the scene to go.

> When you acknowledge a person, you demonstrate a recognition of their value and importance

This is no different than him simply ignoring me. We don't do that in improv, and it's certainly not part of a mindfulness mindset.

Improvisers listen with interest and intent. We are trained to pick up every bit of information provided to us by our fellow players, so we can respond and enthusiastically to move the scene forward.

In short, the practices of mindfulness, in conjunction with our improv practice, allows us to make interesting and exciting discoveries about ourselves and each other!

Imagine the kind of world we can create by not only knowing we matter but truly believing in ourselves and supporting one another.

Be mindful.

Your Take-Aways:

- *The more mindful you are in our improv work, the more mindful you can be in your life.*

- *Be in the present rather than thinking about all of the other things in your head.*

- *Everyone wants validation. We all want to know we matter. We must be present in the moment and acknowledge.*

Chapter 8

Quieting that Pesky Inner Critic

Our inner critic is that irritating little voice in our head that routinely attempts to sway us away from anything outside our comfort zone. In doing so, it prevents us from reaching our dreams and full potential. This negative and often debilitating private dialog we have with ourselves causes us unnecessary and unneeded grief.

We've all heard it rattle off hindering statements in an attempt to knock us down...

"I can't do this."

"I'm going to sound stupid."

"Nobody is going to like this."

"I'll never get a laugh."

To an improviser, those statements are just as bad as going into a job interview with the mind chatter asserting, *"I'll never get this job."* You cannot present confidence when this caustic devil is on your shoulder.

These negative Jedi mind tricks can quickly turn into self-fulfilling prophecies if we allow them to do so. When you step on an improv stage, it's important you demand this smart aleck to take a hike. The last thing you need in a scene is allowing destructive dialog to get into your head.

Fear is nothing more than *misplaced attention.* The inner critic thrives on perceived fears. We must focus on redirecting it.

Our thoughts, whether real or vividly imagined, significantly influence how we feel and behave. When added to our historic negative thought patterns, negative self-talk will covertly lead us on a quiet path to self-destruction. And, as I discussed in Chapter 4, it's all happening under our consciousness radar. Your inner dialogue will either power your success or prevent you from reaching your full potential.

While your inner critic can help you recognize areas where you desire to improve, insensitive and adverse self-talk will cause your performance to suffer and reduce your chances of reaching your goals.

Improvisers listen with interest and intent. We are trained to pick up every bit of information provided to us by our fellow players, so we can respond enthusiastically to move the scene forward.

When first on stage, many new improv students exhibit performance anxiety, commonly referred to as "stage fright."

While it isn't pleasant, it is completely manageable if we don't give it authority over us. Performance anxiety comes from *excessive self-focus*. The fact is, you are hardly ever judged by the audience! They are more likely cheering for you and accepting of your mistakes, blunders or miscues. After all, it's all about being funny, and when screw-ups happen, they are laughing with us. Both the audience and players are smart enough to see the humor in our mishaps.

If you are overly critical of yourself, you're not alone. Most people experience the inner critic's attempt at nurturing self-doubt and negative self-reflections.

Whether on stage, applying for a job, in a team meeting or addressing an audience during a presentation, practice taming your inner critic. Mute the negativity and coach yourself in a productive and helpful manner. You don't have to be a victim of your own verbal maltreatment!

Here are a few simple steps to tackle negative thoughts while developing a more constructive dialog with yourself...

Let go of outcomes.

Many of us are finding ourselves strangled by what I call "the planning instinct." This is many times the hardest part for some people to let go of. When undertaking a project, we naturally have the result we desire in our minds. We want our party to go without a hitch. We want our new photos to look the best, the meeting to start on time, or the Hawaiian vacation to be perfect.

However, the problem is that the more particular we are of the final result we expect, the more likely we are to be disappointed. In life, just as in improv, things seldom turn out as planned.

Develop a conscious awareness of your thoughts

Unfortunately, we are used to hearing (and sometimes believing) our own often negative self-narrations. In doing so, we have become unaware of the subconscious messages we're sending ourselves.

> *The improv muscle, once exercised and toned, will assist you in taking fast, bold and decisive actions in your life*

Be conscious of what you're thinking about. Become cognizant of the fact that just because you "think" something doesn't mean it's true. Our thoughts are many times exaggerated, subjective, and inconsistent with our real-world, real-life sense of being.

Challenge the thought

Thoughts are just thoughts, nothing more, nothing less. Experts estimate that our minds think between 60,000 –

80,000 thoughts a day. That's an average of 2,500 to 3,300 thoughts per hour! (However, I can't prove this as I lost count at 102).

When you find yourself obsessing about a negative thought, ask yourself:

> *Is it meaningful?*
>
> *Is it valid?*
>
> *Is it true?*
>
> *Is it necessary?*

If it isn't needed, forget it and replace it with a thought that's more useful...

Change the thought

For visual folks like me (we tend to think in pictures), consider mentally changing the picture. Distort the negative picture. If it's in color, make it black and white. If it's big, make it small. This is a common practice in *Neuro Linguistic Programming (NLP)*.

Stop reflecting and replaying

When you do happen to make a mistake or experience a bad day, don't replay the events over and over in your head. This only exacerbates the negative thought process.

When you find yourself reflecting and replaying, avoid telling yourself "not to think about it." Like the time-worn adage, "don't think of a pink elephant," the more you try to avoid thinking about something, the more you're likely to focus on it. In psychology, this phenomenon is known as the *ironic process theory,* whereby methodical attempts to suppress certain thoughts actually make them more likely to surface!

Instead, distract yourself with an activity. Go for a walk, organize your desk, or start talking about a different subject. In doing so, you will halt self-debilitating thoughts before they spiral out of control.

Ask yourself what advice you'd give to a friend

If your best friend expressed their own feelings of self-doubt to you, you would never tell them that they can't do anything right, they're stupid, or they don't know what they're talking about. Instead, you would offer them compassionate words of encouragement and advise them things are not as they see them.

Knowing this, why are we so quick to say those things to ourselves? Treat yourself with the kindness you'd demonstrate to your friend. Provide words of encouragement to yourself.

Examine the evidence

Recognize when your thoughts are melodramatically negative. Examine the evidence that both supports as well as refute this thought. Draw a line down the middle of a legal pad. On the left side, list all the evidence that supports your negative thought. On the right side, write down all the evidence that refutes the negative thought. Now study the real evidence on both sides of the argument. In doing so, you can observe the situation with more rationality and less emotion.

Replace disparaging thoughts with more truthful statements

When pessimistic thoughts enter your mind, convert them to a more rational and credible statement. For example, if you find yourself thinking, "I can't do anything right," replace it with a more sensible statement, "I do things really well most of the time, but sometimes I don't."

This statement rings very true with all of us. Every time you find yourself thinking an overly negative thought, respond with the more accurate, "finely-tuned" statement.

Consider how bad it would be if your thoughts were true

We often envision a modest situation turning into a cataclysmic tragedy. It very seldom does. The worst case is rarely as bad as our misguided brains forecast it to be.

For example, if you predict that you're going to embarrass yourself when you're on stage improvising, ask yourself the question, "how bad would it actually be?"

Even if you did happen to feel embarrassed, would you be able to recover, or do you believe it would tragically be the end of your career? Your life? Always remind yourself that you can handle problems.

And with improv, it's even easier because your fellow players always "have your back."

Balance

There's a substantial difference between telling yourself you're not good enough and reminding yourself you can always work to become better. Accept your flaws and areas needing to be addressed; give attention to areas you desire to be better in. Accepting your weaknesses for what they are, and that they don't have to stay that way. Acknowledge that you, like all human beings, have flaws; just be determined to remain a "work in progress" as you strive to become better!

Once you become so engaged in the art of improv and focusing on your fellow players, your inner critic and disrespectful judge will take a much-needed break! You'll soon be attentive and flowing in the moment.

Your Take-Aways:

- *The negative dialog we have with ourselves causes unnecessary and unneeded grief.*

- *Your inner dialogue can power your success or prevent you from reaching your full potential.*

- *Fear is misplaced attention. We must focus on redirecting it and being present.*

- *Practice listening with interest and intent.*

- *Be consciously aware of your thoughts.*

- *Avoid "the planning instinct."*

- *Treat yourself with the kindness you'd demonstrate to a friend.*

- *Convert pessimistic thoughts into more rational and credible statements.*

Taking improv classes have truly changed things in my life for the better! I've improved my listening skills, become more creative, and learned to truly just trust myself and those around me. I'm a controlling perfectionist at heart, so needless to say, letting go and just "riding the wave" of life doesn't come naturally to me.

With improv, there's no room for perfection or control, but I've learned I don't need either of those things on stage or in everyday life. I take what's given to me with open arms and add to it from there. Thanks to improv, I'm better at being in the moment and living out of my comfort zone.

Taking risks and delving into my creativity has helped me break the mental fences I've been stuck in. I use the "got your back" mentality as much as possible with those around me, and it's completely changed my work life and all of my relationships for the better.

Improv has allowed me to not just be whoever I imagine, but it's also helped me develop the best version of myself!

Atti Mire
AdmireMakeup.com
Chandler, Arizona

Chapter 9

Failing without Failure

"Success is the ability to go from failure to failure
without losing your enthusiasm."
- Winston Churchill

There are never failures, just revelations! In the art of improvisation, the difference between bold improvisers and the average person is how they respond to perceived failures.

In improv, as in life, failures are necessary to learn. No matter how hard we try, failures will always be a part of our lives. The discovery of new ideas and directions are cornerstones of the failing process and a necessity in our process of growth. Our thoughts of failure most often trump our desire to try, and we remain in our habitual and silent debilitating patterns of our snug little comfort zone.

Unlike what we're taught, failure is not the opposite of success, it's a stepping-stone *towards* success. There are many motivating stories of highly successful people who have experienced failure as a fundamental part of their pathway to success. Those who have done extraordinary things in the world will praise the importance of both learning from and rising from failures. In the world of entrepreneurship, failure - and the ability to recover from it - are respected merits.

Dr. Seuss's first manuscript was rejected by 27 publishers before eventually selling over 600 million books.

Personal development guru Tony Robbins was rejected by twelve banks before finally getting a measly $1,200 personal loan he needed to attend a Jim Rohn seminar. After attending, he was determined to follow in his mentor's footsteps and went on to inspire and motivate millions of people.

Colonel Sanders was rejected hundreds of times before finally launching Kentucky Fried Chicken and making his fortune in his 70s.

J.K. Rowling was rejected by 12 publishers before becoming the first author to earn over a billion dollars from her famous Harry Potter series.

Oh, and did you know at one point in his life, Michael Jordan didn't make his high school basketball team? Even with that detrimental blip on his radar, he went on to become one of the most iconic athletes of all time.

The common denominator with all of these success stories is that no matter how many times they heard the word "no" or felt as though things weren't working, they persisted. Despite all of the rejections, they never gave up on their dreams and continually pushed until they finally reached the breakthrough they were after.

When I started my auto custom painting business at age 16, I was told I couldn't do it, once by my high school assistant principal (who told me to stop drawing pictures and get my nose in the books so I could go to college) and once by a cute girl I had a crush on. Fortunately, I was a positive thinker and ignored both of them, contrary to what many 16-year-olds would have done. Countless people have given up on their business idea because someone they respected said it couldn't be done.

We all love to talk about our success stories, but we're less likely to discuss our failures and roadblocks that were present and essential in reaching those success stories. Let's face it, as human beings we don't like to be wrong, make mistakes, or look stupid. Those devious thought processes were planted into our brains when we were children. We were taught to be hyper-aware of the perceptions of what others will think of us. We have all subconsciously locked into those experiences of being laughed at when we floundered with an assignment in front of our grade school classmates.

In improv training, we develop a welcoming feeling towards our errors. We embrace mistakes as gifts (see Chapter 18). I've witnessed scenes taking a complete change in direction – all from what was initially deemed to be a mistake – and ending up stronger than the direction it was going prior to the slipup!

Improv forces everyone to work as a team, and I don't know

of any magical process that can accomplish that without making a few mistakes. Mistakes allow us to reconnect to our playful nature and embrace it as a welcome relief in our not having to "get it right" all the time.

Failure is a motivating and guiding principle in improv. Make mistakes and fail big!

Improv pushes us gently past our comfort zone and into the magnificent world of co-creation. It's only when we take the small risks in those "ah-ha" moments that we discover the true gifts of improvisation. By embracing and learning from our mistakes, we learn how to better connect, communicate, and collaborate under the pressure of a live audience.

Have you ever considered getting applause for your failures? We do! In my improv class, I request that students stand up and briefly tell the class about a failure or mistake they made during their week. After they express it, they are required to take a grandiose "tah-da" style circus bow, while the remainder of the class enthusiastically cheers for them. Keep in mind; it's not the celebration of the failure; it's embracing the risk that created it!

Failure is a motivating and guiding principle in improv

We often fear failure so much in our careers that we avoid

taking risks. We fear our fellow team members will think our project idea is stupid, so we don't voice it. When, in reality, our suggestions are pathways to thoughtful solutions and alternative strategies.

We must begin to notice where we stop ourselves and, instead, begin to experience what it feels like when we don't put the brakes on. When we do this in a playful way, our true nature, expression and creativity come alive!

It's better to "guess-n-test" than to overly pre-plan. When I conduct corporate training or lead an improv team retreat, I use exercises that force our critical thinking minds to step aside and trust our instincts – all without the fear of the need to get it right. When we cheerfully experience the feeling of failing in an energetic, fun and supportive way, we discover how to abandon critical thinking and enjoy more stuff in life! We reorganize our relationship with mistakes by embracing them as essential learning opportunities, all in a climate of openness and kindness.

In a show, if an improv player exhibits signs that they are feeling ashamed or embarrassed, audiences will also pick up on it and become uncomfortable. However, when the audience notices that the player isn't disturbed by their mistake, the audience also recognizes that it's acceptable for them to enjoy the blunder as well! For a good example of this, watch some old *Carol Burnett* shows. Their many improvised segments and flubs are priceless learning opportunities!

When we get eliminated from a silly improv game, our fellow students provide a double hand clap and the phrase, *"you are... outta here!"* to their fellow player. The eliminated player then gives the class an authoritative wave, accompanied by an exaggerated "failure bow" as they leave the stage. We must enjoy our mistakes and understand that they truly aren't that big of a deal. Just be careful, however, as mistakes are not a hall pass for sloppy attention (See Chapter 13).

Celebrate yourself for the failures you have made (and will continue to make) because they validate the fact that you're a powerful risk-taking machine!

Now let's get creative!

Your Take-Aways:

- *There are never failures, just revelations.*

- *Failures are a necessary tool for learning.*

- *Make mistakes and fail big!*

- *Don't pre-plan... "guess-n-test!"*

Chapter 10

Creativity... Intelligence Having Fun!

We all desire to exercise our wonderful imagination. However, due to the many negative influences in our lives, we haven't had the opportunity to exercise those atrophied creativity muscles!

"Think left and think right and think low and think high.
Oh, the thinks you can think up if only you try."
– Dr Seuss

When people discover I teach improv, they often say, "Oh, I couldn't do that, I'm not creative." You may be one of these people who question your own creativity. I have news for you... you are indeed a creative person!

Creativity is one of the cornerstones of an effective improv player. However, many people believe they are not creative. There's nothing further from the truth.

Everyone is creative.

The dictionary definition of creativity is "the use of the imagination or original ideas, especially in the production of an artistic work."

I don't necessarily agree with that definition, as creativity is something that's unique to each of us. One doesn't have to sculpt a statue or render an oil-painted landscape to show "artistic work."

In life, we creatively connect ideas and processes into a project. We use creativity in our abilities to manage our budgets to obtain a better return on our investments. We creatively simplify processes to save time. We creatively direct staff members with particular talents to maximize results in our company's sales and marketing efforts.

This known, it's best not to lock yourself into the thought of being a non-creative type. Instead, ask yourself...

> *What position, role, function or activity best allows me to see what others may not?*

> *Where am I able to offer light where others only see the darkness?*

> *What do I understand that others do not?*

What you'll discover is that what may seem blatantly obvious to you is a true gift to another. You'll quickly identify areas where your creativity sparkles!

Creativity is an essential tool for almost every circumstance we experience in life, from solving a complicated problem to thinking of a new angle to increase productivity. Unnecessary and debilitating negative feedback from others has reinforced our misguided desire to "get things right" and not "make a mistake."

This can lead to creativity shut down and cause us to suffer from what I call *imagination deficit disorder*.

We must learn to embrace such impulses and not worry about whether our ideas, statements and actions are deemed "good" or "bad" or if there was "something better." Instead, we must access our imagination by overcoming our fear of making mistakes. We must engage our curiosity by giving our creative muse a kick in the pants!

You are indeed a creative person! However, if you feel like you're "stuck" or missing that creative chunk of you, here are some things highly creative people do. You are likely doing them but just not recognizing them as "creative."

They take advantage of their most creative time

Unfortunately, today's lifestyle seems to incentivize people to become workaholics. Long hours are often seen as what's necessary to "pay one's dues" to success. Though we can reach success through excessive work, in the long term many of us will burn out. It's better to work the hardest whenever you feel the best. Whether early in the morning or at night, find the right routine for your creative tasks.

Improv players, like many creative people, have a place they call the "zone." By discovering your zone, you'll be getting things done on time. Don't worry if it's at the last minute. It's been said the greatest inspiration is the deadline! As an improviser, you'll soon discover that you're more "with it" than you may have previously thought!

Early hours are a common thread with creative people. As I am writing this, it is 4:00 AM on a delightfully warm Monday morning in Scottsdale Arizona. Just me, my notebook, my dogs and my trusty cup of chai tea. Most writers and other creative souls find the early morning's "waking mind" ideal for creation. I certainly do.

Creative people exercise their mind muscles by going with the flow and getting lost in their work. This allows them to banish outside distractions and get things done. However, both your brain and body need rest; time to recuperate and relax. By doing so, the stage becomes set for greater creativity. I have a friend who takes an ice-cold shower late in the evening. He says that after doing so, he feels most creative and often stays up past midnight exercising his creativity. Different strokes for different folks!

They meditate

Meditation is highly prevalent with many creative people. A

few minutes a day of introspective thought will improve the brain's skills in thinking creatively. If you haven't practiced meditation, I would highly advocate giving it a try. I recommend Wayne Dyer's meditation exercises. Check them out on YouTube or in his book, *Getting in the Gap.*

Try a little meditation and mental clearing before delving into your improv class, handling a new client, attending a meeting or most anything coming up where creativity is required. Take a beat and realize there are no dead bodies, so there's no reason to be stressed out!

They recognize they are bored procrastinators

As creative people, we can be easily bored. This is because our minds are always in need of something to engage in. We can be the world's most diligent procrastinators. We're easily distracted.

Thankfully, improv fixes that.

There's no time for boredom or procrastination when your stage partners are relying on you for your creative, energetic energy to move a scene forward.

They have a strong appetite for new experiences

Did you know Einstein was a violinist and would take his violin with him when he travelled around the world?

Creative people have an active mind and need several ways to feed their creativity. See, that's why you have an interest in improv! Don't restrict your creativity to one single outlet. An effective improv practitioner will always look to express themselves in as many ways as possible, discovering new avenues for creative and artistic expression. Go out and experience something new so that you have experiences and adventures you can later describe. Participate in a poem writing class. Take painting lessons. Learn how to lasso.

All inspired paths lead to deeper creativity!

They are challenged with boundaries and rules

As creative souls, we are often challenged with boundaries and rules. Unfortunately, many of us are routinely doing what we don't like. From a job that doesn't nourish our soul to having to deal with someone else's problems, these mental anchors can weigh us down and rob us of our creative fuel.

Now I'm not recommending you quit your job or blatantly break the rules at the office, but just be aware of the constraints that challenge your creativity and adjust them to be less demanding.

Know what you like. Do what you like

Know what you like. Do what you like. Recognize what gets your creative juices flowing. Reorganize any of your life's situations that are causing you stress or preventing you from expressing yourself.

Fortunately, improv has only a few rules (that are highly flexible). And boundaries? Well... they don't exist!

They take risks, fail, and learn

The ability to fail, as well as the acceptance of failure, are both enormous parts of our creativity. No one is a master on their first attempt at anything, so the keen ability to deal with failure and learn from your mistakes are essential if you want to succeed in improv... and life for that matter.

New improv players get disheartened after feeling they failed in a scene; however, seasoned players know that their ability to embrace failure is paramount in getting to the success of the scene. I've witnessed many scenes where it appeared it was about to tank, only to watch it take another direction and be wildly entertaining!

Improv players never set themselves or their fellow players up for failure but vigorously embrace it when it rears its head. The learning experience from mistakes is significant in fueling future scene creativity. Whether on stage, in a meeting or working on a project with your team, step up to challenges. Be friends with failure. Be ready to take risks. Don't limit yourself. Press ahead. Go out on that proverbial limb!

They embrace daydreaming

Daydreaming is one of the most influential habits a creative person can have. Daydreaming allows our imagination to have free rein within our brains. Unfortunately, daydreamers have negative connotations in our society. This is because daydreamers are perceived to be unproductive and/or unintelligent.

That's bunk.

When allowing your brain some downtime, you can significantly improve your creative abilities. Never be worried or ashamed if you find yourself daydreaming. You are allowing your brain to do what it does best – think creatively! Let your mind wander and see what it comes up with. We do it in improv, and so can you!

They are curious

Curiosity is vital to a highly creative person. Experienced improvisers take in all of their surroundings and draw inspiration from everything. New experiences are important opportunities for improvisers, as it provides them more inspiration to draw upon. For example, if you're on stage, and a scene comes into play where you are a baker and you've enjoyed baking as a hobby, you're all set! The more we've experienced in our life, the more our minds will have the ability to naturally create.

They have confidence in their creativity

Many people feel they aren't creative. This is often because they attach creativity to things like painting, singing, sculpting or other artistic endeavors.

Everyone has creative competence. It's the lack of confidence that's holding us back. Our confidence was eroded early in life when we were told our ideas or approaches weren't "good enough." Because of this, we have little conviction in our creative abilities.

I routinely see this in my improv classes; the new student is shy, nervous, afraid and lacking confidence on stage. A few classes later, they're confidently out of their shell and sharing amazing gifts with their fellow players!

Those who express confidence are those who exhibit a greater level of success. Having confidence in your abilities is also interconnected to your ability to fail. By being confident, you are more likely able to embrace criticism and negative feedback while compliantly learning from your mistakes.

Confidence is necessary to move forward with your ideas - even in the face of criticism. There aren't many mistakes in improv, just opportunities to move forward in a powerful way!

They aren't afraid to question things

To be creative, you must be curious. Creative people are always asking questions and seeking answers. The more questions you ask, the smarter you will be, and, as a result, the more creative ideas will surface!

Though it's historically been portrayed as a sign of weakness to ask questions or admit, "I don't know," it actually requires a lot of confidence to request assistance. The more you open yourself up to constructive criticism and attention to detail, the more creative you will become!

The best improvisers understand they need *guidance.* They are humble, understand their limitations and realize they do not know it all. They realize that when other team members may appear better than them in a given context - perhaps portraying an unusual character or uttering a flawless accent - they realize their fellow player's strength is actually their strength when participating in a scene. They know that talented and multifaceted players are needed for an improv troupe to be successful. They provide more opportunities for your own gifts to be discovered!

They follow their dreams

You are infinitely more likely to be creative in an area you truly enjoy than an assignment you have no real desire for. You can always find love in any work you do; however, most creative personalities choose to follow the path of their passion, no matter how difficult it might first appear to be.

Improv gives you an opportunity to escape the rigors of your daily routines and embrace the unknown. The ability to think and act creatively comes down to having a grasp of yourself and the best working practices for you. You must have the confidence to challenge yourself, take risks, follow your dreams and learn to deal with failure when it arises.

No one cares to fail, but it's part of the dynamic process of learning. Improv permits you to learn from your mistakes and often progress to an unexpected but impressive outcome!

"You can't use up creativity.
The more you use, the more you have."
- Maya Angelou

See, you ARE creative! Now embrace it and put your creative strengths to work in your life.

Your Take-Aways:

- *Everyone is creative.*

- *What may seem blatantly obvious to you is a true gift to another.*

- *Take advantage of your most creative time.*

- *Meditate.*

- *Find ways to feed your creativity. Know what you like; do what you like.*

- *The experiences you'll learn from mistakes will fuel future creativity.*

I have lived my life with the idea that, if it scares you, then do it! Nothing scared me more than talking in front of a group of people, but now I can't wait to get up on stage every chance I get!

I started doing improv in 2016, two years later I moved to Los Angeles to study sketch comedy and writing at Second City. I have been lucky and performed on stages at Second City and UCB. I have been a part of a few sketch groups with amazingly talented individuals.

I will always love and encourage others to join improv because as a performer it sharpens your edges and keeps you thinking. Improv forces you to be open minded when you feel closed off. It will continuously make you a better listener because your scene partners are counting on you.

Hannah Heard
Comedian/Improviser
Los Angeles, California

Chapter 11

From Blah to Ta-Da!

You punch the clock and do what you're told. That's the gist of the average worker's daily routine. Nothing special; we got stuff to do. And because of our extensive list of things to "get done," we have little time for our co-workers, colleagues, team members and sometimes, personal relationships with our life partners.

Sure, we occasionally engage in idle chit chat or share a brew during happy hour; however, when it comes to our work, real relationships with our co-workers are few and far between.

It's been said that we spend so much time thinking about what we have to do *next* that we miss what needs to be done *now*. We're so caught up in our to-do list that we fail to creatively step outside the lines and take advantage of the hidden relationships surrounding us every day. We miss many potential exchanges and collaborations that could make our jobs and lives easier. New ideas, experiences, circumstances and suggestions fail in being carried out. Instead, we blindly follow our daily routines. They're safe and accepted – often with fairly predictable outcomes - so why rock the boat, right? Plus, stepping outside those lines could possibly expose us to "bad decisions," even resulting in a "big mistake," right? Maybe one so big that the rest of the staff will talk about us around the water cooler during their breaks. Uuugh.

These "worst-case scenario" thoughts keep us trapped in our routine way of being. We must remember, however, that these are merely old, rehashed thoughts and not real-world experiences! Stepping off the "edge" and outside of your comfort zone is where the results reside.

"Why not go out on a limb? That's where the fruit is."
- Mark Twain

Take the time to recognize your daily patterns of acceptance to circumstances. Question "what is." Think about it, if it weren't for progressive thinking, we would still be in horse and buggies or, worse yet, still using flip phones.

Start paying more attention to creatively engaging with others during everyday mundane activities. Whether exchanging simple hellos, checking out at the grocery store or bantering with the server at a restaurant – seek to step away from common responses and behaviors.

Take time to immerse in unique dialog with colleagues at the office. In doing so, you will modify automatic and routine patterns of communication. You will experience a fresh and renewed interaction with others. In doing so, they will feel acknowledged and heard.

This brings us to the next element of improv, the importance of *Roles and Objectives*.

Your Take-Aways:

- *Recognize your daily patterns of acceptance to circumstances.*

- *Stop thinking about what you have to do next and focus on what needs to be done now.*

- *Discontinue blindly following your daily routines.*

- *Step away from common responses and behaviors.*

- *Creatively engage with others during everyday mundane activities.*

Being exposed to improv classes have made my acting skills more versatile and dynamic.

The experience had me thinking faster, acting and reacting "on command" in a matter of seconds. It forced me to make sense … even out of what I initially perceived as "nonsense."

Improv training has definitely taken my acting to the next level. I feel more confident as my creativity has opened up tremendously. I have also used it in my businesses as well. Clients love my "improv'd" assistance!

Claudia Rubio
HollywoodStylePhotobooths.com
Phoenix, Arizona

Chapter 12

The Often-Ignored Roles and Objectives

When on stage, in a meeting or addressing an audience, we must be conscious of both our *role* as well as our *objective*. We must also be aware of the environment we are in and how that environment plays into each.

In improv, our role is *how we fit into the scene,* and our objective is *how we do our part in moving the scene to a logical conclusion.*

The improv environment requires us to add information to the scene; otherwise, we have no place in it. This is akin to a staff or team member remaining quiet and bringing nothing of value to the table - no ideas, suggestions or direction.

In addition to listening to the verbal dialog uttered by their fellow players, the improviser studies everything else in the scene - the environment, physical traits, energy and distinct lines - all while building from everything they observe. Improvisers must not be focused on where they "want to go," as they will fail to define their role in a given scene. They miss fully embracing and taking advantage of the many possibilities in the environment. They neglect a lot of the obvious (as well as unconventional) qualities that can make the scene considerably more enjoyable for the audience.

We must do the very same thing when engaged with our colleagues, co-workers or life partners.

Perceptual Psychologist James Gibson says that 90% of the information reaching our eyes is lost by the time it reaches our brain.

Yep. True that.

Our eyes see something, then our brain takes over and assembles the details of what we see based on our past experiences. In essence, we construct our perception of reality. Our sensory receptors receive information from the environment, which is then combined with previously stored information about our world that we have built up as a result of experiences.

90% of the information reaching our eyes is lost by the time it reaches our brain

Our perceptions of the world are postulations, based on our past experiences and stored information!

As a magician, I see this playing out when I ask an audience member to "replay" what they just witnessed after watching a magic effect. Their reconstruction of the trick's process was almost always entirely different than the actual series of events that took place!

What does this mean for an improviser? We must be uber conscious and immersed in actively "taking in" everything around us. What may be simply seen as an imaginary water glass on a table can lead to a variety of interesting results. Create a sense of environment from the object. Engage and involve your curiosity. For example, you could be at a bar with an old buddy you haven't seen since grade school, at a birthday party, conversing with another parent at their kid's baseball game, screaming at the opposing team, having a heated argument with your partner. The glass's content can be poured on your head, dumped onto the ground or thrown across the room. There are many options with common objects introduced into a scene, so why settle for "just" drinking a glass of water when it can instead unfold into an interesting passage?

For the improviser desiring to increase their talents, get accustomed to practicing effective object work (see Chapter #21). It will add imaginative realism and creative expression to your scene! Creating a sense of environment from a simple object will quickly take your performance to a higher level of creativity.

Seeing things for more than they initially appear can increase the potential and possibilities of most everything in our life, relationships, team and business. Become a more astute student of your environment. It will pay off on stage as well as in life!

Make your routine "blahs" into impressive "Ta- Da's!"

Your Take-Aways:

- *Your objective is how you do your part in moving a given situation to a logical conclusion.*

- *Embrace and take advantage of environmental possibilities.*

- *90% of visual information is lost by the time it reaches our brain.*

- *See deeper into things - they are more than they initially appear to be.*

- *Become a perceptive student of your environment.*

Chapter 13

The Lost Art of Active Listening

I'm sure you think and truly believe you're a good listener, right? After all, you have to be if you desire to participate in conversations, don't you agree?

However, the real question is... are you an *active* listener?

One of the popular improv games is *String of Diamonds*, whereby a group of a dozen or more improvisers are lined up. The first person starts a story with a simple opening sentence, such as, *"once upon a time in a small village..."* while the last person in the line suggests the ending sentence, such as, *"... and that's when I realized I was on an alien aircraft."*

Now the story begins with the first person, with each participant player adding a single sentence. The aim of the game is to build a comprehensive story as it goes down the line. It can get quite outlandish, often causing players to grasp at ideas as to what "their sentence" will be. The participants toward the end of the line must actively listen to their former players as they must segue the earlier sentences into a logical conclusion as it relates to the alien aircraft.

Active listening simply means what it says, listening actively. That is, rather than just passively hearing the speaker's message, fully concentrate and focus on what is being said, verbally and non-verbally.

Even though active listening is one of improv's foundational skills, its importance is often not effectively communicated in improv basic training. Unlike passive listening, which is the act of hearing a speaker without retaining the full message, active listening permits engagement and recalling specific details without needing the information repeated.

Active listening involves *listening with all senses*. It's an acquirable skill that can be nurtured and grown with practice. The use of active listening skills is not only essential in the world of improv, but it's also an influential tool for strong teammates, effective leaders and successful presenters. Developing this skill will help build and maintain relationships, solve problems, improve processes and retain information.

Sadly, however, most people aren't very good at active listening. Most are listening to reply instead of listening to understand.

Let me say it again...

Most people are listening to reply instead of listening to understand.

During improv scenes, active listening is a required and refined ability to focus and engage completely with our fellow players. We must understand their message, cues and body language while comprehending the verbal information on the surface. In doing so, we are better able to provide a more thorough and thoughtful response in creatively moving the scene forward.

Attentive, active listening is a valuable skill in life, just as it is in a scene on the improv stage. Unfortunately, our cluttered minds have reduced listening to simply *waiting for our turn to speak again*. Active listening is becoming a relic in today's fast-paced world.

To successfully build a scene or conversation with a fellow player, you must aggressively listen to the offer they are giving you while integrating bits of it into your response. Many times, a player will miss critical information in a scene that could have taken it to a more creative place. As a result of their oversight, the scene becomes boring, frustrating to watch and annoying to fellow performers. If you are planning on what you want to say or what you desire to happen, you will almost always miss out on important information delivered by your fellow player. *You must attentively listen to what others are saying.*

When your fellow player recognizes that you're an active listener, they will feel more confident in taking their time when delivering their information. This is because they know you aren't going to step on their words with unwelcomed interruptions. When you interrupt your fellow players, you are telling them you are either not listening, what they are saying is irrelevant to you, or you think your idea is better than theirs.

Collaborative relationships cannot be built on interruptions.

Someone who is not listening or, worse yet, attempting to be funny by delivering their own joke, can destroy a scene.

A good improviser is quick on their feet, actively listening and paying attention to every detail coming their way. They not only listen carefully to everyone in their troupe, but they also make sure they're communicating clearly and effectively. Competent teamwork includes both active listening and efficient communications. Together, they accomplish impressive results.

Active listening also benefits us in our persuasion, influence, and rapport building skills. In the context of our business or career, those skills are vital. As demonstrated in an improv scene, the more we can link what we say in response to what another says, it makes for a more focused and directed conversation.

Whether on stage or in the office, if you have a good idea and desire to see where it goes, you must be clear and concise. For example, if you wanted to launch an improv scene about a little clown car with dozens of clowns coming out of it, you wouldn't vaguely say to your fellow player, *"Hey, look at that!"* A more effective statement would be, *"Oh my, look at that little car! I can't believe all of those clowns fit in there!"*

The latter communicates that you are launching a dialog about a clown car, whereas the former doesn't give your partner any details about where you desire to go. Communicating clearly and efficiently about what you need is important, as your fellow players won't know what you need until you ask for it!

Be attentive by paying attention!

Stay present in the scene or conversation. Make a conscious effort to commit to hearing and being respectful to your conversation partner.

In improv, we must be in the moment. By doing so, we support our fellow players, are fun to perform with, deliver more detailed scene elements and effortlessly move the scene forward. Be open and flexible to what your fellow player or conversation partner is expressing. Reflect on what was said *and reserve the urge to jump in too soon.* Pay attention to both verbal and non-verbal cues.

In improv, scenes can go in many different directions, so it's best to withhold early judgement. Once you've paid attention to your partner's verbal and non-verbal cues, it's time to demonstrate the prized rule in improv, the "Yes, and..." rule (coming up in Chapter #15). That is, *accept what was delivered and build upon it.*

In my improv classes, I developed an exercise called *"I heard you say..."* Two players engage in conversation, starting each of their sentences with *"I heard you say,"* then repeats the information their fellow player just cited while adding additional supportive dialog to it...

Player #1:

"My dog has been itching a lot lately..."

Player #2:

"I heard you say your dog has been itching a lot lately. You may consider bathing him in 'No More Itches' shampoo..."

Player #1:

"I heard you say I should try "No More Itches' shampoo..." that's a great idea. Maybe it'll work for me too, as I've been itching a lot..."

Player #2:

"I heard you say you've been itching a lot – perhaps YOU may have fleas..."

This exercise normally continues longer than my example, and it forces players to actively listen, while still formulating short verbal responses.

In performances, I recommend players utilize this practice by connecting their partner's statements to their responses by using simple word connectors...

"I understand..."

"I see..."

"Yes, that makes sense..."

"I agree..."

These are all forms of "yes, and..." responses.

Be conscious of and practice non-verbal skills as well. Non-verbal elements can assist in active listening while adding more realism to an improv scene. Use them. Occasionally offer your fellow player a supportive nod. Smile or provide a facial response, aligned to the direction of their words. Be aware of your eye contact and movement. Avoid distractive movements and gestures while they're talking.

By adding non-verbal techniques into scenes, they will appear more natural and, as such, more believable and entertaining to the audience.

Because active listeners are highly engaged, they're better able to recall specific details in a scene. Effective communication skills are advantageous, not only on the improv stage but in our world as well. The ability to clearly communicate instructions, ideas and concepts is truly a rare asset.

You will discover that the study and practice of improv also assists in those often-uncomfortable, unarranged conversations that show up. From an unexpected question during a presentation to uninvited criticism, your training will position you in the right state of mind to handle the unexpected. You'll be grounded and credible instead of panic-stricken!

Whether you're on stage, interviewing for a new job, discussing a promotion, working with fellow team members, presenting information to an audience, or in a management role, improving active listening skills will assist you in more critical thinking and conflict resolution.

Put active listening to work!

The first step in active listening is accepting your fellow player's offer. That's next!

Your Take-Aways:

- *Attentive, active listening is a valuable skill in life.*

- *Listen to understand, not to respond.*

- *Collaborative relationships cannot be built on interruptions.*

- *Active listening simply means listening actively.*

- *Listen with all senses; be conscious of and practice non-verbal skills.*

- *Active listening benefits you with persuasion, influence, and rapport building skills.*

- *Being respectful to your conversation partner.*

Chapter 14

Hey, Make Me an Offer I Can't Excuse

Every improv scene starts with a player making an *offer*. These proposals can be lines of dialogue, gestures, or locations of a scene. Offers are pieces of valuable information. This is the reason improvisers call them "gifts."

An offer is anything one says or does that move the scene forward or gives direction as to where things are going.

Offers are construction blocks to fascinating passages and the driving force behind an effective improv performance.

The receiving player always eagerly accepts these offers and expands upon them. The stronger and more defined the offer, the better it is for your team member. This is because you've given them more to work with. The offer is the paint, and the scene is the canvas!

The best offers should carry a large degree of *Specificity* (See Chapter #19), and if an object is involved, *Object Work* (See Chapter #21). The more detailed the offer, the more the scene will unfold with imaginative particulars. This makes it easier for your fellow players. Further, it assists the audience's ability to follow along.

Well-delivered offers must flow freely - without hesitation.

There are weak offers and there are strong offers. A weak offer is ambiguous or vague and fails to move the scene forward. Be clear and concise with your offers; don't incoherently ramble to the point your team member doesn't know what you're talking about.

Be certain your partner understands the information you're providing to them. For example, if your scene partner indicates their character isn't feeling well in a scene, an ambiguous response would be,

> *"Here, this will help you with that..."* [while extending
> your hand as though you were giving them something].

Your partner gives you a blank, deer-in-the-headlights stare— the gaze of total non-comprehension. You are forcing your partner into bailing you out of your vagueness.

An effective improviser recognizes their blunder and would and quickly add more information...

> *"My mom told me that if you eat this ginger, your
> belly ache will go away..."*

By better communicating more specific information – a stronger offer – the scene can now move forward in a more focused and creative way.

Making a strong offer is what brings home the bacon. In improv, we call this taking a *bold action*. Take a look at these two scenes:

Scene example #1:

Player #1:
"Hey Bill, I bet you are excited for your first day on the job at the bank!"

Player #2:
"Yes, my father worked at that bank for many years."

Scene example #2:

Player #1:
"Hey Bill, I bet you are excited for your first day on the job at the bank!"

Player #2:
"Yeah, I sure am... I plan to get the combination to the main vault, grab the cash and head to the Bahamas with my yoga instructor."

Which one sounds more enticing? Which do you desire to hear more about? It's obvious which one is weak and which is strong. The strong offer demonstrates a bold action.

Please understand, this response isn't delivered in a joking way, but instead articulated in a serious "I plan to do this..."

kind of an *Oceans Eleven* fashion. A strong offer should *never* be delivered as a punchline.

Unlike the vague, weak offer, the strong proposal forcefully moved the action forward, opening up a marvelous pathway for a creative scene to unfold.

The other player could then respond with something like, *"I'd love to help you; I've always wanted to rob a bank, but I'm afraid of guns."*

> *A strong offer should never be delivered as a punchline*

You can see that can set the scene for planning a bank robbery, with one of the potential robbers fearing guns, instead of an uninteresting scene about a new bank employee.

Another example:

"Good morning, Dr. Hagerty."

This vague offer presents only two uneventful pieces of information – it is taking place in the morning, and the player is a physician named Dr. Hagerty. The audience and fellow players recognize this scene to be likely taking place in a hospital.

But it's just not juicy.

A more enhanced offer would include more information and a "twist" in the scene:

> *"Good morning Dr. Hagerty. The prisoner has been prepared, and the courts have indicated we may proceed with his lethal execution."*

Now we have the makings to launch this scene into a more unique environment. Your fellow players now have a lot more to work with.

When opening a scene, it's important to deliver variety and uniqueness with an interesting twist. In this example:

- It could be that it's Dr. Hagerty's first day on the "job."

- The prisoner could plead that he's not the one who committed the murder.

- The assisting nurse could be the prisoner's bitter ex-girlfriend.

Starting the scene with a thought-provoking twist can launch an otherwise mundane scene into a variety of interesting directions!

The same rule of exercising effective offers applies to our lives as well. Think about it... are you more attracted to a detailed offer or a vague offer? If you're buying a new car, are you okay with the salesperson giving you generalities about its features or the benefits those features provide to you? How do you feel when your team member brings ambiguous or confusing ideas to the project table?

Details matter.

Whether on stage, in the office or attempting to sway your children or partner to see things your way, be cognizant of your offers. Make them bold, concise and easy to understand. In doing so, their acceptance will be more motivational.

Now let's talk about the importance of the *acceptance* of the offers...

Your Take-Aways:

- *The best offers (in life or improv) must carry a large degree of specificity.*

- *Your partner must understand the information you're providing them.*

- *Be cognizant of your offers; make them bold, concise and easy to understand.*

Chapter 15

Yes, I Accept Your Offer!

Skilled improv players are working without a script and revere being in the moment. They are continually developing their sense of focus and engaged imagination, and it all starts with *agreement*.

With the assistance of fellow players doing the same thing (and a little luck), it will always lead to an interesting scene. Through bold teamwork, everyone is committed to their partners in collaborating to achieve impressive results. Theatrical improv has a number of simple rules that must be followed. The most famous is the *"Yes, and.."* rule, or the *Rule of Agreement*.

This rule suggests that players must:

1. agree with the reality their scene partner is creating

2. add additional detailed information to that reality.

An example of agreement banter between players:

Player #1:

"Let's go to the Dinosaur Museum."

Player #2:

"Yes, I love those mega monsters... I'll bring my camera."

Player #3:

"Yes, and I'll bring my grandmother... she may recognize some of them!"

These players are accepting the gift while contributing another component to move the story forward.

If a fellow player rejects the other player's reality, the scene usually stagnates and becomes stymied by conflict. For example, if my scene partner says, *"Hey Mike, let's go skydiving,"* and I respond with, *"I'm not Mike,"* the scene swiftly dies. This is referenced as denying or blocking in the improv world (I'll have more on this in the next chapter).

Instead, suppose I just go along with my partner's gift and "be Mike." I engage in conversation around skydiving and in doing so, we can quickly get to more stimulating particulars, and a more detailed, energetic scene will start to develop.

You always accept what is given (the "yes" part) and build from whatever is provided to you (the "and" part). No matter how bizarre or outlandish the gift may be, as a fellow player, you must be obligated and honored to accept it and move the scene forward.

Saying "yes" to an open-ended suggestion may first appear to be thrusting you into a quick, unknown future, a leap of faith into the abyss of uncertainty. It requires complete trust, open-mindedness, and the willingness to give your ideas away with no attachments. However, the brave and optimistic improviser will always commit themselves to the power of the affirmative response!

Improv players embody the Rule of Agreement. When they hit the stage, they snap into improv thinking. They keenly focus on their fellow players' statements as well as details of the scene they present. This peripheral focus quiets the inner critic and frees up their creative mind to be imaginative and uninhibited. They're ready to say YES!

You will often be required to abandon your preconceived ideas and, instead, get behind your partner's idea as though it was your own. In the same manner, they will vacate their ideas in getting aligned with yours. It's a different approach but a powerful one. Exercising the "yes muscle" builds optimism and hope. It's an act of bravery and optimism. In uttering an affirming "yes" statement, you share control of the scene with your partner, while making them happy in return!

Our brains actually enjoy saying "yes" to new discoveries!

Beyond the standard "Yes and," there are other offers of agreement that are just as effective...

"You bet..."

"You're right..."

"Sure..."

"Okay..."

"Of course..."

"I'm with you..."

"Good idea..."

Avoid the NOs. Again, I'll have more on this in the next chapter. For now, just understand that it's not cool to negate in improv. We've been denied enough in life, so there's isn't a need to bring "no" to the stage. Instead, discover and exercise the power of "Yes."

To become a good improviser, we must let go of the fear of being seen as weird, bad, or wrong. The thought of, *"What will people think of me if I say that?"* is an immense stumbling block for not only the improviser but people in general. Many of the ideas that once seemed weird are ones that have changed the world!

As I discussed in Chapter #5, studies have proven that improv training actually shuts down the part of the brain that's responsible for self-censoring. This is a good thing as it means that in situations requiring quick decisions, you will not second-guess yourself but will instead find it easy to contribute ideas to assist in finding a solution to whatever challenge is being experienced.

The Rule of Agreement is a cornerstone element of improvisation; however, its benefits can also be appreciated in our careers as well. Once embracing improvisation with like-minded fellow players, you'll discover the power of affirmatively working together on stage and how this process spills over into your everyday life. Whether in a staff meeting or on stage, agreeing with your partner, team member or colleague begins a building process. There is a spirit of "having one's back" and cooperating with others!

Great improvisers joyfully let go of the future and focus on being present in the moment. By doing so, they learn to disregard one of our most fundamental human instincts, *they avoid thinking ahead.*

Due to the ever-changing scene environment in improv, there is no future. Well, there is, but we just don't know what it entails! A good improv scene is like a game of ping pong... without the points. You serve, they return. They serve, you return.

You must authentically communicate how the current moment feels, no matter how awkward or uncomfortable it may be. I once quipped this "gift" to a fellow player in an opening scene, *"I'll never forget that time we were at Nordstrom's, and you had diarrhea on the escalator."*

You have to be ready for anything in improv!

In this scene, my fellow player used the power of silence in his response. He waited, looked at me sheepishly and said, *"You had to bring that up..."*

Accepting and agreeing with your fellow player's offers almost always brings natural funniness to the scene. Since effective improvisation is not about one's sharp wit or comic ability, a good improviser is one who is not self-centered, mentally awake and routinely acts upon impulses to say or do something useful to move a given situation of circumstance toward a resolution... and it all starts with the spirit of "YES, and!"

The Rule of Agreement is effective in the workplace as well. A "yes" response will continue building the conversation while "no" shuts it down. In life, as in improv, ineffective ideas are just steppingstones to good ideas.

As we discussed in Chapter #13, you must be *actively listening* to every word a partner is providing you in a given scene. Things move fast on stage and without focused training in active listening, many players miss critical auditory elements of the scene. Audiences hear it, and if the player didn't, audiences pick up on the inconsistencies.

The same holds true in a meeting with a client, sharing ideas in a team meeting or having a conversation with a friend... *one must intensely listen to everything.* After improv training, it's very common for the "yes, and..." rule to be introduced as a remedy to workplace negativity. They discover that it's okay to dismiss the safe and simple "no." Instead, team members agree to follow a "yes" idea in the moment to see where it goes. In doing so, communication is improved, and acceptance is increasing through the reduction of barriers.

When you habitually meet situations with an energetic "yes," the mysterious energy of agreement transforms the way people perceive you! Confidence is quickly amplified. Think about it... people who aren't confident seldom contribute, so everyone loses. It's about a new infrastructure of communicating and connecting.

To experience the power of "yes, and" in your life, select a person you know and care for to experiment with. Choose to say YES and agree to everything for a full week. Agree with all of their statements, ideas or recommendations. Consider their thoughts and opinions ahead of your own. Allow them to have the stage. This will also assist you in becoming more creative with your answers. If you truly disagree with a statement, by first agreeing, you'll find your disagreement being eventually addressed but in a more pleasant, non-adversarial and distinctive way!

For example, if a friend offers you a huge piece of chocolate cake on the first day of your diet, your response could be,

> *"Thank you! I've just started my new diet, but I'll put this in the fridge for my very first cheat day... I'm looking forward to it!"*

This is an affirmative approach. No denying. No refusal of "the gift."

So, now you know... the number one rule improv is the "Yes, and..." rule. Through the pillar of acceptance, you establish trust and mutual respect. Just as in life and business, quick adaptation to ever-changing criteria, finicky clients and a demanding boss are all commonplace. Always strive to build on another's ideas and offer suggestions.

Improv teaches you to think quickly, be confident and move things in a positive direction. Couple that with affirmative responses, and you'll create more expressive scenes as well as improved communication.

The aura of gratitude is ever-present between effective improv players as they recognize the importance of not only working as a team but stepping up when a fellow payer is struggling. Before improv shows, it's common practice for the players to pat each other on the back while saying, *"got your back!..."*

And they truly mean it.

Powerful life lessons are built into the "yes, and..." rule. The next time someone shares their idea with you, remain open-minded and accept it. Even if you find fault with it, begin by accepting it as viable, and *then add to it*. Saying "yes" keeps us open to possibility and with more possibilities, we discover limitations are removed! It's your reality, and in your world... things are whatever you and your team players desire it to be!

Whether on stage, at school or in the office, the "yes, and..." rule will allow you to accept anyone's idea, build on it and make it even better!

Your Take-Aways:

- *Agree with whatever the gift may be.*

- *Add additional information to that reality.*

- *Abandon any preconceived ideas.*

- *Let go of the fear of being weird, bad, or wrong.*

- *A "yes" response will continue building the conversation while "no" shuts it down.*

- *Ineffective ideas are just steppingstones to good ideas.*

I started taking Improv for fun, but soon found I gained collaborative skills that were very instrumental in acting auditions, on stage and in the office.

I learned how to actively listen and respond on the fly, which came in handy for my work in stand-up comedy. It also boosted my confidence as I learned to make bolder choices.

Since improv is a team sport, I especially look forward to the camaraderie social aspects!

Dean Florence
Actor/Comedian
Cave Creek, Arizona

Chapter 16

Don't Be a Block Head

Failure to say yes in an improv scene is called *blocking*.

Saying no is the ego's way of attempting to control the future. It's our brain's historic way of trying to *control* the situation instead of *accepting* it. Many people are so used to saying no that it has developed into a standard reaction. Most of us are not consciously aware of our negative habits.

As outlined in the previous chapter, effective improv requires each player to understand and adhere to one brigadier rule - the *Rule of Acceptance*. Failure to do so is referred to

> *Saying no is the ego's way of attempting to control the future*

as *Blocking* or *Denying*. The moment you break the Rule of Acceptance, the action ends.

For example:

Player 1:
> *"Hey Mike, let's go to the water park today; it's half price Monday!"*

Player 2:

> *"No, I don't like water parks."*

Player B just killed the scene; there's no place to go. It's their inner critic offensively desiring to have it "their" way.

We block when:

1. *we say no*

2. *we think we have a better idea*

3. *we fail to actively listen*

4. *we simply ignore the situation in a scene*

Blocking surfaces when the detractor in us attempts to take over the show. Our vile habit of saying "no" is just a way we attempt to control the future. Further, when we block others, we're blocking ourselves as well.

The Rule of Acceptance declares that no matter what happens on stage during a scene, each player must *accept it as real.* We don't have to like it or believe it, but it's our obligation to accept it. Many times, it's not where we may think the scene *should* go, but we understand that acceptance is required to *allow it to go where it's going.* Saying yes and following through with added information to move the scene forward prevents us from blocking. When accepting, we don't deny its existence. Acceptance means to comprehend something as it actually is – *a recognition of facts.* We must recognize and accept the current reality of what's taking place.

Whether entertaining an audience from the stage, managing staff members, contributing to our team's efforts in resolving a challenge put before us, or whenever something happens in our lives, which we do not (or cannot) control, we must accept it. If the Rule of Acceptance is broken, the scene croaks. However, if all players accept, agree and go along, the scene continues and creatively unfolds. The doors then open for most anything!

There's a slight twist to denial – a rule "breaker" if you will. That is, you cannot deny facts of a scene; however, there are opportunities to deny the *premise of* or an *opinion within* a scene.

For example, if two players are carrying out a scene, and one appears to pull out a knife, their fellow player would normally accept the fact that they have appeared to bring a weapon into the scene. They can't deny or simply ignore it because their fellow player has creatively introduced it. You cannot say, *"that's not a knife"* to your fellow player, just as you wouldn't say that to a thug who pulled a real knife on you in a dark alley. That's denying a *fact*.

However, if your fellow player doesn't specify it as a knife, a viable and more creative response could be, *"What are you going to do with that banana?"* The player can then take the object (the banana) away from the "robber," peel and eat it while continuing the dialog. The robber can then be positioned as a confused grocery store manager who just got fired from his job. This twist in the scene can open the door for funny dialog!

This may first appear as denying; however, it really isn't. The player introducing the weapon didn't say, *"I have a knife."* He just pulled it out, perhaps with dialog like, *"put your hands up."* Our brains then fill in the rest of the story... e.g, *"oh, he has a knife or gun..."*

We didn't deny the presence of a knife because it wasn't introduced as a knife. Instead, we altered the *premise* of the scene, and in doing so, took it into a funnier direction. *Many times, these new directions are better than the direction they were originally going!*

Another example:

Player #1:

"Here, I brought you peach pie."

Player #2:

"Uuugh, peaches cause me to break out in hives!"

You're not denying the fact that it's a peach pie but denying the *offer*. A denial of fact would be, *"That's not a peach pie; that's a chocolate cake."*

See the difference?

Denial in Life

Outside of improv, we cannot live in a world of denial. We

can't deny a medical condition, addiction or failed relation-ship. Denial is always the result of a bad decision. Don't be stuck living in denial. Always remember that you can make affirmative decisions. Just as we do in an improv scene, be willing to accept what is put before you, and build upon it.

We've experienced a lot of negativity in our lives. A UCLA sur-vey found that the average one-year-old child hears the word 'No' more than 400 times a day! This may sound like an exag-geration, but it's not. When we tell a toddler *'No,'* we often say, *"No, no, no!"* which is accentuating the negative message three times in a matter of seconds! If you were like me as a child -active, curious, inquisitive and daring - you likely heard it even more!

If you have children, be aware that these negative expressions are far from an encouraging way to raise a happy, self-reliant kid. It damages their long-term self-confidence and self-esteem. Misdirected childhood experiences have resulted in many undesired consequences in our adult lives.

Don't be the person who finds "no" a viable or appropriate re-sponse. Just as in improv, observe how you not only speak to your children, your partner, or your fellow workers but also how you speak to yourself - inside your own head. Be positive and inspiring. Those who find "Yes" to be a more suitable re-sponse are rewarded by adventures. Those who say "No" merely remain with the safety they were already experiencing. There's no fun in that.

Life seldom carries itself out exactly as we desire. While we have every right to attempt altering it, we cannot deny what it brings forth. We must accept whatever is happening at a given time. Living in a world of denial means you've not adhered to the Rule of Acceptance.

It's an easy fix, though, just step away from denial and begin accepting! It's a more enjoyable way to experience the roller-coaster of life!

Now, let's get back to improv...

Your Take-Aways:

- *Saying no is the ego's way of attempting to control the future.*

- *When we block others, we're blocking ourselves.*

- *We cannot live in a world of denial.*

- *Misdirected childhood experiences have resulted in undesired consequences in our adult life.*

- *Life seldom carries itself out exactly as we desire.*

Chapter 17

Huh, You're Questioning Me?

An important component of good improvisation is...

Avoiding questions in scenes.

In improv, every detail is a choice. If you avoid committing to a choice, decision or detail, you are avoiding doing your part, and the scene will indeed suffer. In a scene, questions are devoid of value. If you are asking a question, you're generally not contributing to the conversation. Questions are a lazy way out, placing the burden of creativity on your scene partner to fill in the information. That's not fair.

As with most rules of improv, there are exceptions. Good questions that energetically move the conversation forward are okay, and I'll discuss the exceptions in a bit; however, it's always the safest bet to avoid them. Instead, it's better to provide direct statements. Note the difference between these two opening sentences...

"Hey, who are you, and what are you doing here?

"Hey Mike, I haven't seen you since you won that hot-dog eating contest at the county fair!

The former places burden on your fellow player to assemble who they are as well as a scene location. The latter takes away that unfair burden from your fellow player and offers them a place to go.

Many amateur improvisers attempt to start a scene with the statement, *"What are you doing?"* This is like saying, *"I'm lazy and not comfortable in taking a risk, so I'll let you manage this scene."*

Improv players must stand up, be bold and take control...

> *"Hey, Jimmy, I see you've been workin' out...*
> *looks like you're building a nice set of guns there..."*

Now you have a scene that can go somewhere. Your scene partner has been provided a gift, practical information that can be built upon. This is considerably more respectful than meekly asking what he is "doing." New improv students tend to introduce questions into scenes. This is because they are nervous or feel they can't think of anything to say.

There are five types of questions that will hinder a scene:

Open-ended questions like:

> *"Who are you?"*

> *"What's that?"*

> *"What do you need?"*

> *"What are we doing here?"*

Open-ended questions put unfair pressure on their scene partner to assemble a response.

Closed-ended questions are those that can be answered by a simple "yes" or "no." Closed-ended questions are commonly used when the player has some idea of what's going on in the scene but desires clarification. For example,

> *"Are you the refrigerator repairman?"*
>
> *"It sure is cold down here in the basement, isn't it?"*
>
> *"Do you think Mary will babysit my guinea pig
> while I'm on vacation?"*

Leading questions are questions that suggest the answer. Leading questions actually bend the improv "no questions" rule a bit. They do so because you are actually making an offer and in doing so, there is a lot of places for your fellow player to go. For example,

> *"Mom, I know I'm not very smart; do you think it's
> from Dad's side of the family?"*
>
> *"Officer, if I promise not to speed for the rest of my
> life, will you let me go without giving me a ticket?"*

Loaded questions are questions other players may attempt as a nervy way of forcing their idea forward. For example, if a player desires their scene partner to be pregnant, they would pose the question:

"Are you going to the doctor about your morning sickness?"

Loaded questions are the ego's lame attempt at controlling the scene and should be avoided at all costs.

Repeated questions fail to add details to a scene but only echo dialog that's already been delivered. This also happens with new improv players when they don't know what to say. It is glaringly obvious to the audience when it occurs.

> *Don't be lazy in a scene. Avoid questions*

Player 1:

"I'm feeling like I'm going to be sick."

Player 2:

"You don't feel well?"

Player 1:

"I'm going to get a gym membership."

Player 2:

"Are you going to start working out?"

Again, like other rules of improv, the "No Questions" rule can be creatively broken. Questions are part of human interaction and, as such, can creatively open or bring real spice to a scene. Some examples:

Will you go to Home Depot and get me a shovel, so I can bury someone?

Did you ever put a dead body in the trunk of your car?

Did you seriously think I wouldn't know that you emptied the bank account?

How did your blind date go last night?

Be aware when questions creep into your brain during a scene. If you discover yourself asking one, add "because" at the end and convert it into a bold statement. Here's an example using the previously mentioned instance of a repeated question...

Player 1:
   "I feel like I'm going to be sick."
Player 2:
   "You don't feel well... because... you drank too many margaritas at the casino last night."

Don't be lazy in a scene. Avoid questions. Convert them into a more enticing statement. Your partners will be grateful for your efforts!

Your Take-Aways:

- *Avoid questions in scenes.*

- *When you find yourself doing so, add "because" and convert it to a statement.*

Improv Class? What is that? I can't do that. Improv is for really clever, funny people. Yet, I found myself in a class, terrified and being told to get on stage my very first time. Joe Hammer, the instructor at the time, could see the fear in my face, shrugged and said, "You know some words, right? Use some... that's it."

Fast-forward three years, and now I'm doing what was once my very secret dream... Stand Up Comedy! Yes! I'm a working comic! I've been inspired and totally jazzed by pro improvisers. I watched, listened and eventually performed with them, each time getting better and more trusting of the basics of the art.

The positive feeling of knowing your fellow players would always "have your back," and every idea or statement would be greeted with an energetic "Yes, and ..." These are the building blocks I learned, along with... "make it fun!"

By listening carefully, I got a deeper understanding of how improv affects your whole life! I now have Parkinson's Disease and need a way to rattle my brain, keep the memory muscles strong and LAUGH! Laughter is truly the best medicine there is, and I will continue to take improv classes as long as I can; it's a giant part of my life!

Chris Cluff
Comedian
Phoenix, Arizona

Chapter 18

Mistakes as Gifts

In the world of improv, mistakes come with the territory. They are influential tools for better understanding. The goal is to correct them while learning from them.

"Try. Make mistakes. Fail big and fail happily. If the audience sees you unbothered by your mistakes, then they can enjoy them too, but if they see you feel humiliated and ashamed, they will be uncomfortable."
- Keith Johnstone, Pioneer of Improv Theatresports

If you're not making mistakes, you're not doing anything. Learn from them, and move on! Be decisive. Take ownership and commit to your choices. Look onward, not backward. Be positive. Remember, it's always more powerful, influential and persuasive to say what you do want rather than what you don't want. It reminds me of the old adage, *"don't think of a pink elephant."* It's an unreasonable request.

When it's your turn to add to the scene, you must act quickly (unless the scene calls for a brief silence or pregnant pause). You must add something relevant, clever, and maybe even funny, but you must get out of your head and reject any ideas that are thought to be "not good enough." Improv requires *decisiveness*, and you must utter the first thing that comes to your mind, and it doesn't matter if the result of your decision is a bit obscure.

Your partner will have your back and assist in building your response into the scene. Just as in life, one cannot just make irrational choices; however, as humans, we tend to over-analyze. Most decisions are superficial in nature, and one choice wouldn't impact the overall result over another. You're only wasting time by over-analyzing. In improv and in life, just make a decision, and move on.

During my years of teaching improv to kids and teens, I always included games that were designed to make failing outrageously fun. These were the most popular, confidence-building exercises we did. Once they realized they could not do it wrong, and mistakes were all part of the fun, they blossomed in their personal expression and creativity.

I was once in a scene where I was a supervisor of a restaurant crew. Early in the scene, I referenced a fellow player by a wrong name that was previously introduced. I immediately recognized my error, so I gently shifted my character to an ego-centered idiot who didn't care about the people who worked for him, calling them the wrong names or tagging them with offensive labels like "Skippy" or "Cute Buns." The crew members would correct me, but I condescendingly ignored them and continued the behavior.

The truth is, *screwing up is part of the improv learning process.*

Many great inventions were either based on or resulted from mistakes.

Through his experiments with his invention of the light bulb, Edison didn't assert attention to his many failures, but instead, chalked them up as theories that simply didn't "prove the truth." He risked being seen as a disappointment among his peers and didn't give any thought to the possibility of his invention ending as a failure.

New improvisers always make mistakes. However, if they aren't trained to respond to these mistakes as gifts, the results can be agonizing for the audience to watch. The same is true in life, the boardroom, or with your sales team at the office. Imagine transforming mistakes into gifts. Would you feel differently if you knew mistakes would be embraced? In improv, that's our standard operating procedure! Being "in the moment" is exactly what it's about. When a mistake surfaces, effective improvisers focus on that mistake. We don't gloss over it. We explore it to find out why it happened and how it can help. There's a lot of fun and education in playing with those unexpected slipups!

Being fearful of mistakes is something we've been taught since childhood. We were taught that there is always one right answer. Mistakes often resulted in our being chastised in front of our classmates, or a low test score on our exam would provide adverse consequences on our report cards.

Our world strives for the elusive concept of perfection. We're taught the importance of "getting it right." We've become blunder phobic – fearing our mistakes are going to make us appear that we're less than we desire to be. Then we move on to our careers where mistakes are frowned upon – many times to the point of letting down our fellow team members, demotion or even losing our job.

Before you know it, fear of making mistakes becomes our reality. Our internal dialog chimes in with self-judgement, further reinforcing the fear conditioning through self-attacks...

"They're going to think I'm stupid."

Pulling from hundreds of negative events from our subconsciously-stored historic recordings, our mind's power to self-assault is merciless! Our anxiety rises when we even think of making a mistake!

As these mistake-centered events occur in our lives, we eventually begin developing strategies to avoid making them - everything from becoming a perfectionist to simply being afraid of attempting anything outside of our comfort zone.

What we fail to realize is that mistakes are gifts of growth. Without them, we would never achieve any new accomplishments in our life.

Many people are caught up with what I call *"The Passion of*

Perfection." It's beyond being a perfectionist; it's the stagnating process of doing *nothing*. It's our failure to act, due to internal negative dialog, self-criticism and the fear of doing something wrong.

People experiencing this problem are aware of it but can't seem to shake it. They start a myriad of self-incrimination questions, like, "should I do [insert action plan #1] or [insert action plan #2]?" Then they'll go on to unearth invented problems, challenges and difficulties related to both of their possible choices. Often, the result is inaction and simply staying with what is the status quo.

And with that, there is no growth.

Failing isn't the colossal setback our minds have made it up to be. It's the lack of training in techniques to move forward after failing that holds us back. Everyone screws up, but if you demonstrate that a mistake doesn't define you, and you're capable of moving forward, then others will follow your lead and move forward as well.

After only a few improv classes, most discover that they couldn't imagine their lives without it! Not only for the fun but the fact that its lessons can be applied to our lives as well as our career, relationships or business.

In improv, we embrace mistakes as opportunities. Given the spontaneous nature of improvisation, mistakes do happen... and quite often. The key is getting past them and moving forward to a logical (and hopefully humorous) conclusion.

Errors cannot be avoided in life. The positive side is that they are necessary as they provide growth, rethinking and redirected actions to reach our desired result. Much like an aircraft that's set to autopilot; it is consistently making course corrections to reach its destination.

I've seen major blunders in improv shows; situations where one player is not paying attention to what their fellow player is doing. For example, let's assume the audience gives a one-word suggestion for the scene, and that the word is *"monkey."*

Immediately and without any fraction of forethought, both players come out as monkeys. Outside of screeching, grunting and picking bugs from each other's hair, once these players landed on this response, there isn't anywhere to go. Their sophomoric thinking and premature decision left them little room to improvise.

More experienced improvisers would not revert to such an obvious response to the scene, but instead, bring a more appealing and energetic approach...

Perhaps one player can set the scene as an "accelerated evolution" story. In doing so, they narrate the process of evolving from primate to human. The other player picks up on the direction, accepts this reality and follows along, demonstrating their fellow player's story, initially speaking in caveman grunts, perhaps even ending "the evolution" as a boastful politician!

Alternatively, the initial scene could entail one player as a senior staff member at the zoo, assisting the other player on their first day on the job at the monkey exhibit. Or possibly a monkey-handler, who is attempting to place a spider-monkey on the shoulder of a zoo visitor who exhibits a deeply-rooted fear of primates.

By players initially discounting the obvious when the topic is announced, creativity will come into play for a much more enticing and engaging scene.

Mistakes are gifts, doorways to a new adventure. This perceived "mistake" of both players choosing to be monkeys can be converted into an enjoyable and funny scene if the players are conscious of the error and commit to the progression of the scene.

The obvious choice is seldom the best choice.

Improv is all about accepting and building. If my partner asserts that I'm a deranged magician who always wants to show off my magic skills, then yes, I am indeed that character. I am obligated to create a reality based on that statement.

Improv also assists us in adapting quickly to change. Its very existence thrives on suggestions from the audience or the troupe's director. Once "out there," these suggestions immediately initiate thought processes with the players. The suggestion can be ideas for a scene, a character, or perhaps an action. Let's say the suggested word is "dancer." In your head, you are prepared to enter the stage as a professional dancer, ready to show off your skills on the stage floor. That is until your fellow player suddenly quips,

> *"My mom sent me to this dance class; I'm so glad*
> *you are my teacher!"*

So, before you can express the little predetermined dance number in your brain, you're suddenly thrust into the part of playing a dance *instructor*. Yep, your witty dance moves are gone; you're now responsible for teaching dancing to your fellow player! You ruthlessly eradicate your pre-conceived thoughts and notions and immediately adapt... and with a positive attitude. You now are required to move the scene forward, expressing the 'Yes, and' rule...

> *"Yes, and I look forward to showing you the dance*
> *moves I taught Michael Jackson..."*

As in most of life's challenges, there is always more than one direction to take. And there is *never* one right answer in improv.

On the other side of the coin are those who could less if they made mistakes. That's just lazy, and they won't last long in improv. I once had an employee like that. When confronted with an obviously avoidable error, his response was, "*Nobody's perfect.*"

Sure, that's a very true statement; however, when simple mistakes are continually made because of one's failure to recognize the consequences of their actions and instead just blindly move forward, then it's a different story.

I once asked him, "*Mark, how many babies do you think they drop in the delivery room?*"

He looked at me puzzled, "*None,*" he said awkwardly.

"*That's correct,*" I replied, "*the reason is that they realize the severity and consequences of their mistakes. Sure, nobody's perfect, but they are trained to take precautions before the problem occurs. You can do the same thing.*"

He agreed, and his frequent errors in judgement were soon greatly reduced.

Don't strive to live in an imaginary world of perfection; however, don't foolishly act without a bit of defined thought. Take a beat before taking action. Pause. When a mistake occurs, avoid self-punishment and blame, make adjustments, and move the scene forward.

Improv scenes and stories are born from players' innovative imaginations, but as I often say to my students, "*If you dig a hole, I'm not saving you.*" For example, if you start the scene by establishing your partner as a serpent-like space alien that eats only eggshells and lives in tunnels under Disneyland, then you're responsible for owning up to all those details. It won't be easy, but you'll quickly discover the result of your pointless attempt at being funny will backfire. *What you've made difficult for your partner swiftly becomes just as difficult for you as well.*

Don't go there.

Always set up your partner for success. The way you desire and expect your partner to rely on you must be equal to the way you rely on your partner. Remember when your parents told you to treat others the way you desired to be treated? Jump in and offer them a gift – a practical statement that cleanly moves the scene forward and keeps the story fresh.

This same lesson applies not only to the improv stage, but even more so in the workplace. To be an effective team player, qualified leader or reliable colleague, your team must trust you. They must trust that you'll do your best to complete an assignment. You'll have their backs in demanding situations while offering support as it's needed.

In life, just as in an improv scene, it's not about being perfect and avoiding mistakes; it's acknowledging the mistake in an accepting, non-defensive way, learning from it and moving the process forward to achieve an even better result. If you screw up at home or at the office, admit it, be humble and responsible, then get back to the task at hand. Learn something, and move on. We all respect accountability, and often, the times we screw up make the best stories!

"Failure is the only opportunity to begin again, only this time more wisely."
- Henry Ford

Remember, *mistakes are gifts; don't fear making them.* Respond to them without negative self-criticism. Find the opportunities hidden within them. Transform and redirect them into a positive life experience. Celebrate them!

Your Take-Aways:

- *If you're not making mistakes, you're not doing anything.*

- *Screwing up is part of the improv learning process.*

- *Being fearful of our mistakes is something we've been taught since childhood.*

- *The obvious choice is seldom the best choice.*

- *Pause. Take a beat before taking action.*

- *Mistakes are gifts; don't fear making them.*

I've been doing improv comedy for over two years, and during that time I've been through a few job searches.

I've found that my experience with improv has positively impacted my interviewing skills more than HR seminars and mock interviews ever have.

As a financial services professional, comedy does not play a large role in my work or conversations around it, but my time with my improv troupe has made me better at communicating stories in an engaging manner and thinking on my feet in responding to interviewers' questions.

Marie Daigle
Business Analyst
Phoenix, Arizona

Chapter 19

Specificity

So what if you can't pronounce it; just be aware of what it is.

Specificity is simply *the quality or state of being specific.*

Vague references deliver vague messages to the audience. For example, if you take on the characteristics of a waiter and welcome your scene partner to a restaurant, each audience member could have a different image of what kind of restaurant it may be. Is it a fast-food joint or a fine dining setting?

However, if you deliver a more specific line, such as welcoming them to *"Cheryl's Diner, the home of Alabama's Biggest Bowl of Country Grits,"* that's a

> *Specificity creates momentum*

lot more specific, and will allow the audience to better visualize the scene.

Improv demands *specificity.* Specificity creates momentum. The more specific a player is, the better the scene will progress. As we discussed, avoid questions and forcing your partner to do all the work. The second biggest blunder is being unclear. By practicing specificity, you will help both your scene partners and your audience members in vividly "seeing the details" of your scene.

Specificity is improv gold. It can make scenes truly come alive.

There is an improv technique called *flashing*, whereby one draws on their own real experiences to create content in a given scene. The technique is quite simple; you embrace a word or the last line of dialogue from your partner to remind you of something from your own life. You then bring some specific aspects of that memory into the scene.

The name of the technique is reflective of the actual process in doing it, as it must be done as quickly as possible. Your brain must be propelled to rapidly recall a memory as it relates to the word or line. Don't try to noodle it too long; just flash back to a moment in time as it relates to the topic.

For example, if someone starts a scene by saying,

"Check out my new car!"

I would immediately flashback to my days in the auto custom painting business...

*"Dude! It rocks! I love that red candy apple paint!
And that deep clearcoat really makes those pearlescent
flakes sparkle!"*

Practicing this technique isn't difficult. Just look at random words and try to rapidly associate them with a memory or specific situation from your own life. In doing this process, you'll start uncovering little details that'll make your scenes more invigorating.

That cigarette becomes a *"filterless camel."*

That cat becomes *"that damn stray that leaves dead mice on my porch."*

That can of soda become a *"Fanta cream soda."*

That rug becomes a *"hand-knotted Persian throw."*

Draw things from your own life, memories and experiences. The beauty of becoming skillful in flashing is that the specifics you generate are unique to your life. Audience members won't know that... they'll just think you're a genius!

I use an improv game called *More Specific*. It's a simple exercise in tuning-up an improv player's specificity muscles. It starts with two or more players talking through a conventional scene. At any point during the scene, I'll call out, "More specific!" When this happens the player's last line must be restated but in a more detailed way.

For example,

"Here, I brought you this cake."

Director: *More Specific!*

"Here, I brought you this pineapple upside-down cake."

Director: *More Specific!*

> "*Here, I brought you this pineapple upside-down cake; I made it from my grandmother's recipe.*"

Director: *More Specific!*

> "*Here, I brought you this pineapple upside-down cake; I made it from my grandmother's recipe – and it took four hours to make, so you'd better like it!*"

This exercise forces our brain to recognize and articulate more specific elements of the scene and, in doing so, we open up new possibilities and become better improvisers!

Specificity can also be demonstrated in other forms, such as size, weight or other physical attributes. If you're holding a bunny, it should appear different than if you were holding a toaster.

It is also demonstrated in *physical actions*. For example, if I'm calling someone on my phone, instead of just holding an imaginary phone up to my ear and start talking, I must make some preliminary actions duplicating the real-life process. I must first take the phone from my pocket. I then give it an ex-aggerated broad swipe to unlock the screen. After doing so, I tap the screen a number of times to launch the call. I put it to my ear. I also allow a brief pause for the ringing before carry-ing out "my side" of the conversation. I may even decide to use a pregnant pause, as if there is no answer, and when I'm about to tap the screen to disconnect the call, the person suddenly answers.

Think about it. That's what happens in real life, so why should it appear different in your scene?

Relate to the *location* of the scene. If you're in a basement, recall your basement experiences. Was it cold and damp? Dark? Weird smell? Did you see a cobweb or a spider? Bring those experiences in!

If you're at grandma's house, reference the smell of that apple pie or the size of those decorative plates on the kitchen wall. And look how big that cookie jar is – wonder if there are any cookies in there? Just come up with two or three things; the audience will fill in the rest through their own experiences.

We operate on autopilot 80% of the time and aren't consciously noting micro experiences in our lives, but it's these things that bring realism to the stage. Your life is a plethora of unique and unusual activities, habits, events, processes and idiosyncrasies. Pay more attention to them. Identify the details in the mundane day-to-day things you do... and bring them to the stage! *Live a more observant life!*

Do you have a friend or co-worker with weird idiosyncrasies? Perhaps a weird eye twitch or strange laugh? Bring them to your scenes as a character trait as well!

Go beyond merely responding to your fellow player. Deliver

some specifics, and watch how it energizes the scene – many times, taking it in an all-new (and more exciting) direction! The more skilled you become at visualizing the details of what you're doing, the more specific you're going to be in describing or pantomiming it.

Specificity, coupled with convincing object work, coming up in Chapter #21, will make you an enormously better improviser!

Your Take-Aways:

- *Vague references deliver vague messages.*

- *Specificity is the quality or state of being specific.*

- *The more specific you are, the better the scene will progress.*

- *Draw things from your own life, memories and experiences.*

Chapter 20

The Secret 55% Communication Tool

The improv stage is simply an empty space that can become anything you desire it to be. It's a fertile environment that exists in the shared imagination of you and your fellow players, therefore you must use all of the communication tools in your tool belt.

Effectively communicating is more than merely bantering dialog on the platform. Improvisation requires the participation of all forms of interaction. There is more than only the spoken word. Much more. 55% of effective communication is our body language (Kinesics), and 38% is our tone of voice (Intonation). Only 7% is the actual words we speak. This known, why would you not implement body movement and varying tones of voice to energize your scenes?

By not actively engaging body language and voice tone, you can be missing up to 93% of your communication abilities!

Ever thought about that?

Improv provides the opportunity to introduce many non-verbal components, all ready to deliver tremendous added value to a scene. Posture. Physicality. Quirks. Facial expressions. The amount and type of eye contact. Object work. They can make an otherwise dull scene come to life!

Improvisers understand that scenes consist of only possibilities, and those possibilities can be more effectively demonstrated through these non-verbal mechanisms. Skills of imagination, emotion, characterizations and body language will all skillfully come together to form a compelling passage. Let's look at a few ways that you can better convey a message in an improv scene...

Facial expressions. Our faces can be extremely expressive and have the ability to express emotions without saying anything. There are six primary emotions: *happiness, surprise, anger, sadness, fear* and *disgust.* Each of these can be powerfully demonstrated through facial expressions. However, each of these emotions can have various forms of facial expressions. For example, you would project a different look of surprise at an unexpected birthday party, compared to the look of surprise when your child took their first steps.

> *Improvisers understand that scenes consist of only possibilities*

Body movement and posture. The way you move and carry yourself during a scene communicates more than you may think. Body postures convey a lot of information. Are your arms crossed? Are you tilting your head? Looking down? Rubbing your hands together? Twisting your hair? Clasping your hands behind your back? Placing your hands on your hips? These all carry a message that will either reinforce or dilute your spoken word.

Gestures. How do you use your hands in a scene? What's different in those gestures when you're angry, arguing or excited? Gestures don't replace what you say, they emphasize what you say. Studies have shown that they can increase the effectiveness of our communication by as much as 60%! I'll list some hand gestures in a moment that will greatly enhance your verbal messages. Use them!

Eye contact. Have you ever watched the eye movements on a person who was being untruthful? The way you look at someone in a scene can communicate many things, and the audience will quickly pick it up. From anger to affection, how you use eye contact in your improv practice can deliver impressive results.

Space. During a conversation, we've all felt a bit uncomfortable when the other person was standing a bit too close and invading our space? Doing so during a scene while your partner is uncomfortably leaning away can deliver an identifiable and funny message! From aggression to dominance, as an improviser, you can use physical space to better communicate nonverbal messages.

Voice. It's not what you say; it's how it's said. The audience hears more than the mere words you speak. They hear the timing, the pace, the loudness, the tone, the inflection. From sarcasm to anger, affection to confidence, the tone of your voice can significantly assist you in delivering clearer and more identifiable messages to both your scene partners and your audience.

Physicality will better assist in projecting more defined scene details and environmental emotions. Whether it's a lost couple seated in a less-than-desirable roadside diner, or two new astronauts in the spacecraft's cockpit navigating their flight to the planet Jupiter, the players are responsible for the scene dynamics, all created at the same time it is told.

As outlined in *The Importance of Effective Communication* by Edward G. Wertheim, Ph.D.,[1] nonverbal communication can play five roles:

Repetition: It repeats and often strengthens the message you're making verbally.

Contradiction: It can contradict the message you're trying to convey, thus indicating to your listener that you may not be telling the truth.

Substitution: It can substitute for a verbal message. For example, your facial expression often conveys a far more vivid message than words ever can.

[1] https://bit.ly/3iKY2jl

Complementing: It may add to or complement your verbal message. As a boss, if you pat an employee on the back in addition to giving praise, it can increase the impact of your message.

Accenting: It may accent or underline a verbal message. Pounding the table, for example, can underline the importance of your message.

Effective communication skills assist us in our life, careers and teamwork as well. The nonverbal communication cues, the way you listen, look, move and react, telegraph to the person you're communicating with if you're being truthful, if you care and how well you're truly listening. When your nonverbal skills align with the words you're saying, it will increase clarity, trust, and rapport.

Here are 10 hand gestures that will greatly assist in delivering a highly focused message. If you are playing a sizable venue, be sure to exaggerate them in a larger way.

Listing. Are you expressing three things that you're irritated about? Count them out with your fingers!

This or that. Talking about two choices? Here or there? Gesture to your right and left.

The backhand slap. An old Italian favorite when you're laying down the facts and want to be heard.

Pinched fingers. The pinched thumb against the index finger gesture is a politician's favorite when desiring to make a strong point. (This is also referred to as the "Clinton Thumb" although John F Kennedy was the first to use it in supporting his message).

Open arms. Fonzie brought this gesture of confidence and coolness to TV on *Happy Days*. *Aaaaay!*

Facepalm. No better way to say, *"I can't believe you said that!"*

Hands up. *"Hey, don't look at me... I didn't do it!"*

The steeple. If you want to look wise and powerful, put the tips of your five fingers together in front of you. We use it a lot in public speaking.

Fist pump. Yeah! You can do it! A fist pump can emphasize strength, encouragement or intensity.

Air quotes. Always funny.

The hand rub. Excited? Anticipating something good that's about to happen?

Hand on heart. No better way to express your sincerity!

The brain tap. Great when telling your scene partner to *"start using your brain!"*

Stop. *"Wait, hold on there... I didn't say that!"*

Shoulder shrug. Great if you don't know or simply don't care.

Finger to chin. Hmmm, maybe you gotta think about it for a while?...

Raised finger. A great way to get attention for your great idea!

Finger tip-tap. But your palm heels together and tap those fingers to be a sneaky mastermind or a neighbor with a devilish plan.

Your Take-Aways:

- *The words we speak are only 7% of effective communication.*

- *Body language is 55% of effective communication.*

- *Tone of voice is 38% of effective communication.*

- *Physicality projects more defined scene details and environmental emotions.*

- *When nonverbal skills align with words, it will increase clarity, trust, and rapport.*

- *Use hand gestures.*

I always had problems meeting new people and forming relationships, but improv has allowed me to connect and trust fellow players during stage scenes. After graduating college and looking for a full-time job, improv has also allowed me to be calm and confident during interviews.

Improv training has also changed my approach as a performer. As a student with The Groundlings and studying with Mindy Sterling, Phil Lamar and Annie Sertich, it has helped me develop strong characters and connections on stage. I have also used improv skills while performing stand up at The Hollywood Improv as well as a guest host with The Night Time Show Live.

Being able to think on my feet has added an increased level of confidence to my performances!

Sarah Salthouse
Actor/Comedian
Los Angeles, California

Chapter 21

The Power of Object Work

Object work in improv is a form of pantomiming the presence of objects with hand and body movement. It physically demonstrates the existence of "real" objects during an improvised scene. This is important, as most improv games are performed without any physical props.

Making the invisible visible is part of the magic of great improv.

Since you don't know where a given scene might take you, it's important to be ready to effectively mime on stage. I'm not referencing white-face miming, where you demonstrate an existence in an invisible glass box or gesturing as though you're pressing against an invisible wall. I'm talking about the times when you may be handed a drink, a cigarette, a pie or a watermelon.

Making the invisible visible is part of the magic of great improv

With object work, you must be ready for almost anything.

While scenes can be funny without doing so, effectively panto-miming an object brings better-defined realism to the scene. Whether you're driving a bus, mopping a floor, stretching piz-za dough or shaving your face, *effective realism is important.*

To become efficient in object work, you must be believable in pantomiming that whatever object you have in the scene is truly in your hand. There's more to doing it effectively than how you've eagerly strummed your air guitar to Aerosmith's *Walk This Way.*

To be truly effective in object work, I recommend you practice by actually "doing something with something you would do it with"... that is, carrying out the process you desire to panto-mime. For example, if you desire to appear to be sweeping a floor, get in front of a full-length mirror with a broom. Now lightly and slowly sweep. Look in the mirror and be con-sciously aware of every part of your body as it relates to both holding the broom and your movements as it carries out the sweeping process. How are your hands positioned? How does your body move? Do it a few times. Mentally lock in the often imperceptible yet visual details. Now set the broom aside and duplicate the same hand placements and body movements without the broom.

As a magician, if I appear to place a coin in my hand, it ac-cepts the imaginary coin with a bit of weight, just as my hand would accept it if I were to truly place it there. I often demonstrate this to my students, explaining how the art of magic relies a great deal on effective object work.

There are also three hidden benefits to object work. That is, *creating a scenario on stage can be a lot easier if you are doing something physical.*

- By keeping your hands busy, you can free up your mind to be more in the moment, thus taking the pressure off the need to think of the "right" thing to say. Instead, it allows you to react more honestly, with believable dialogue.

- It frees you up to move around the stage. Scenes are many times more real and believable when you are moving about the stage.

- It allows you to practice more "showing" over "telling."

The challenge, however, is doing it all in a convincing way. I tell my students to move 10% slower and be 100% *more specific.* Most object work is done too quickly for both your partner and the audience to understand what you are doing. What you think you're doing is more in your head than that you are demonstrating on stage.

Notice how you do little tasks around your house; how you pick up a glass, how you hold it, how you set it down. Notice the weight of it in your hands. Notice how you reach to turn a doorknob, how your hands hold your car's steering wheel. Become a student in looking more closely at everything you do. *It's easier to remember than to invent.* This is how you become proficient in carrying out impressive scenes with object work.

And don't forget the process of obtaining and returning the object. Just as in real life, a broom, mug, or glass doesn't just "appear" in your hand. It must be picked up from a location. Perhaps the broom is leaning against a wall, or the coffee mug is sitting on a table or being handed to you. That known, it only makes sense that when you're done with it, it must be returned to a location. Be sure to practice the retrieval and return of the object as well as the process of using it in a scene. I wish I had a dollar for every scene where a player's cigarette, water glass or shovel magically disappeared from a scene. Uuugh.

Pay attention. When another player has introduced an object into a scene, acutely study it as *they* use it. They may just hand it off to you. If they do, you must carry on with the object's size and weight as well as any other characteristics your fellow player has assigned to it.

Be conscious of *object denial.*

Object denial is a form of denial whereby you ignore an object your partner has brought into the scene. They spend five minutes setting the breakfast table, and you walk right through it. Or they invite you to get into the car, and you walk right through the door. Or they pour you a cup of coffee from the coffee maker, and you later go to that stage location to get something from the refrigerator.

You must not only be listening to your scene partners but astutely paying attention to what they are setting up and establishing visually.

Practice pantomiming one thing and talking about something different. If you think about it, it's what we do in everyday life. When we make coffee, we don't talk about making coffee; we talk about our kid's report card or the upcoming deadline on a work project. You'll recognize increased object work proficiency when you're able to maintain your physicality along with unrelated dialogue.

If you desire to dig deeper and become more proficient in object work, I highly recommend *Mime Spoken Here: The Performer's Portable Workshop* by Tony Montanaro.

Your Take-Aways:

- *Object work in improv is a form of pantomiming the presence of objects.*

- *With object work, you must be ready for almost anything.*

- *Always be ready to effectively mime object use on stage.*

- *Practice by doing something with what you actually do it with.*

- *Stage dialog can be a lot easier if you are doing something physical.*

- *Avoid object denial.*

- *Pay attention to what fellow players are visually setting up and establishing.*

- *Practice pantomiming one thing and talking about something different.*

Joe teaching an improv class member object work

Chapter 22

Conscious Consideration

We love being funny. We love attention. We love the spotlight. That's why we're attracted to the intriguing world of improv! When we're on stage with other players, however, our self-centered, selfish egos often kick-in, and we sometimes turn into competitive little kids, trying to get the audience's attention.

It doesn't work.

Grandstanding is when you're looking to draw attention to yourself, your scene situation or event as it relates to only you.

Don't make jokes – make sense.

When it comes to improvisation, it's important that you be present in the mo-

> *Don't make jokes ... make sense*

ment... without grandstanding. Instead, you must embrace the fine art of making your improv partners look good on stage. No, I'm not talking about straightening their collars or adjusting their hairstyle, I'm talking about giving up the spotlight to them when carrying out a scene. Trust your scene partners; they are your collaborators, and they will actively support you, as you must do in supporting them. Without respecting and supporting our fellow players, we would be reduced to a boring monologue. It's all about having their back, exercising a team effort destined for an enjoyable scene.

Improv players understand and exercise the cardinal improv rule of "making their fellow players look good." You must think about what you can *give* to the scene rather than what you can *take* from it. When all players adhere to this selfless rule and focus on the interests of their fellow players, the scene is destined to be successful.

The challenge for many new improv students is that they feel they are somehow giving up their spotlight and recognition.

It takes time and a robust consciousness to accept this selfless rule and allow your partner to have the audience's attention, however you must be cognizant that they are (or should be) allowing the very same spotlight to shine upon you. Release your ego and make yourself vulnerable. The scene really isn't about you; it's about the totality of the scene circumstances you are merely participating in.

Making your partner look good is a pretty simple process... focus on the sum of scene dialog and events instead of yourself. You may not get laughs, and it seems like a thankless effort, but not only will your partners and audience respect it, but karma will bring the personal benefits back around to you in future shows. At times, that may mean you take a backseat, perhaps only as an emotional support player, feeding straight lines to a well-established character your partner has brought into the scene. There's nothing the matter with that. Have you ever seen Johnny Carson interview Rodney Dangerfield on *The Tonight Show?* Johnny continually fed Rodney lead-ins for his famous "no respect" branding, using questions like *"How's the wife and kids?"* or *"How's your health?"*

Improv players are required to resist the urge to hijack the spotlight and attempt to overshadow their fellow players. When an individual player attempts to capture the spotlight, the humor most always backfires. The audience is mindful when someone is attempting to "steal the show." This is the biggest challenge when stand-up comedians enter the world of improv – they are confronted with the fact they are sharing the stage with others and unable to deliver witty punchlines for laughs.

If you try to be funny, you won't be.

Improv is not stand-up comedy. In attempting to do so, it will appear contrived or forced – sometimes, many times appearing as desperation. The real magic is what makes improv great – instinctually trusting your gut, connecting with your intuition and speaking it! When we give up the urge to show off our talent, our organic wisdom can emerge, and our trustful muses can come forth and speak through us. All of our life's past experiences and circumstances have prepared us for this moment. Attempting to search for a witty line robs us of energetically revealing those experiences.

Our fertile minds are rich with images, ideas, words, thoughts, and dreams. The key is to simply welcome what's there!

Again, you must think about what you can give to the scene rather than what you can take from it. Efficient and effective improv always results when every player's goal is setting up their fellow players for success. Before every improv show, the green room is buzzing with team players patting each of their teammates on the back, making eye contact and saying, "got your back."

This is done not only out of tradition but also because creating a show out of nothing in front of strangers can sometime be a frightening experience. This known, it's important to be reminded that your fellow players are indeed there for you and, above all else, they'll be listening and looking for ways to support you, no matter what happens on stage. Improvising is a truly collaborative art.

The same holds true at the office. When we can trust that our team members and fellow staffers will "catch us" no matter what, we feel safe to be courageous and commit. We will feel comfortable in getting out of our head and pour all of our risky (and sometime outrageous) creativity into the situation, circumstance or challenge at hand.

The more diligent we are in setting up others for success, the better opportunity we have of effectively accomplishing our overall mission. When we're so focused on our own stuff, it costs our team members time and energy, damages our momentum and injures our reputation. It actually has a reverse effect on what we're attempting to accomplish in the overall project.

Set your team members up for a win. Replace any thoughts of competition with thoughts of cooperation. *Cooperate with others; compete with yourself.* Make it your mission to create pathways of success for those you lead.

You'll be surprised what happens when you make a habit of reminding the people in your life that you "got their back." By exploring the unknown, amazing possibilities will become unlocked!

Your Take-Aways:

- *Improv is not stand-up comedy.*

- *Don't Grandstand.*

- *Don't make jokes – make sense.*

- *Make your fellow players look good.*

- *Think about what you can give to the scene rather than what you can take from it.*

- *Cooperate with others; compete with yourself.*

I work in the hotel industry and manage large scale renovation projects that require me to lead conference calls, on-site meetings, and interact with numerous players.

As the project manager, I'm responsible for the overall budget, schedule, and quality, including managing a team of design, construction and management/ accounting professionals.

Improv has taught me to be a better listener, communicator, and collaborator in team environments. Additionally, it has given me better instincts. I am required to make quick decisions and I used to overthink too much. Improv has afforded me more confidence in trusting and running with my first instincts.

Nick DiMaio
Principal, Project Management Consulting Firm
Scottsdale, Arizona

Chapter 23

From the Stage to the Boardroom

Improv has long been considered an important instrument in an actor's tool belt; however, other businesses and organizations are getting in on the benefits of the art as well, discovering that it delivers practical and valued skills into the workplace.

Innovation requires creativity, and improv, by its very nature, is profoundly creative. It ignites fun and passion in those who study it. It sanctions trust and acceptance through a mutual discovery process. It also encourages individual choices, risk-taking and exploration, all robust benefits to organizations desiring those competencies from their staff and team members.

Progressive companies are recognizing how improv can assist their team members by vastly improving their communication skills. Aspects of improvisation can be easily adapted from the stage and put to work in almost any organization. Improv training creates an enjoyable place for bold ideas to emerge and be developed, all *with* creativity and spontaneity and *without* fear or apprehension.

Improv works! From increasing staff resilience to attaining a stronger ability to manage change, reaching higher team building agility, to increasing innovative thinking. *Duke, UCLA, Notre Dame* and *MIT* have all incorporated improv into their class curriculum. In doing so, it has proven to assist future leaders by making them better prepared and more effective at "thinking on their feet." Improv removes barriers, builds understanding and delivers immediate results.

Improv builds trust. Whether in a business or personal relationship, trust is an essential element that's crucial to communication success with your partner, team or company.

> *Trust is the anchoring principle in improv, and it's easily adaptable to staff training*

Trust is the anchoring principle in improv, and it's easily adaptable to staff training. Improv teaches how to overcome fear and use the principle and motivation in "having each other's backs."

Improv builds ideas. Improv's principle of "Yes, and..." opens the door for more expansive discoveries by reducing judgement and encouraging active listening. Using it in an organization will assist team members to expand their ideas through collaboration and innovation. Applying it during brainstorming sessions will encourage free sharing of ideas and also make people feel more comfortable and empowered. It becomes a positive and collaborative experience! There is power in the *"Yes, I accept your idea and I'm going to make it better,"* as opposed to the *"No, I have a better idea"* approach.

Improv improves communication. Improv also provides an easy pathway to better listening skills. When practiced in a fun environment, this soft skill is easier to comprehend. Improv not only teaches you how to deeply listen to what others are saying but also *how* they're saying it. In doing so, you'll embrace non-verbal communication components that assist in getting a more focused message across. The ability to quickly think on your feet decreases reaction times - another element that fares well in organizations whose staff has had improv training.

Improv expands interaction and collaboration. Improv training is an influential tool in developing more diverse communications. Staff, teams and committees will work with a more distinct outlook in achieving their project completions or company goals. Team members will feel more comfortable communicating in a variety of work situations. They will be consciously aware - present in the moment while listening carefully and contributing freely. These skills are also immensely useful in a workplace that relies on adaptability and flexibility.

Unlike conventional soft-skills training, improv bundles soft skills training into an energetic, educational and enjoyable process. Improv will teach acceptance, how to listen better, and how not to fear failure. It will positively affect workplace competencies from adaptability to collaboration, communication to creativity. Companies can also utilize improv training to learn more about their staff's collective strengths and weaknesses. It's no surprise that bringing improvisation training to the workplace is an exciting staff development tool!

Your Take-Aways:

- *Improv is a dynamic tool for progressive organizations!*

- *Improv builds innovative teams.*

- *Improv contributes to rapid problem-solving.*

- *Improv assists staff in responding and adapting to change.*

- *Improv improves leadership skills.*

Chapter 24

Team Building

Progressive organization and management programs have harnessed the power of improv to teach creativity, collaboration and co-creating. The results have proven it can energize teams, surface breakthrough ideas, and enable learning from perceived failures.

Improv is more than just a way to carry out compelling stage scenes with fellow improvisers. It can assist progressive leaders in rethinking how they manage and communicate during their day to day interactions. Improvisers are trained to listen to their partners, embrace failure, cooperate and move a scene forward rather than developing their own agenda.

As you have discovered in *The Improv Edge*, improv training offers us powerful tools and techniques to practice. It delivers a unique and unconventional type of focus. It changes how our brain processes information, unlocking our individual and group potential and creativity.

Improv enables us to be flexible in spotting new opportunities while letting go of what isn't working. Listening, accepting offers, exploring ideas and, most importantly, giving others a chance, helps everyone deal with uncertainty.

When engaged in a conversation about direction, strategy or creativity, people often feel they have to select *one* idea to run with and many times, decide on that idea too early. When an improv scene begins, many elements come into play. It's raw. Unfocused. Non-specific. As it plays out, the focus eventually gets more distinct. No player is in charge or in control. Improv is a very organic and ever-changing environment. You may have a set idea of where a story should go, but you'll quickly have to discard that as soon as you hear what your fellow player has to say before it gets to you. The improviser is never panic-stricken because they know the best thing to do is be with the other person, physically and emotionally.

When given an assignment to resolve a company challenge, a successful team requires harmony and cohesion between the team members. Improv boldly assists in this interpersonal communication skill. It can also assist team members in not feeling the need to land on one initial project path as well. Instead, the process becomes more organic, many times leading to a result that otherwise would have been overlooked using conventional team efforts. Team build-

> *Team building with elements of improvisation makes the process more about collaboration, not competition*

ing with elements of improvisation makes the process more about collaboration, not competition.

Improv players know the importance of making their fellow players look good, and the same holds true with an effective project team. The better they make their partner look, the better the overall scene result will be. I can always tell how much experience one has in improv when they enter the stage with "some really great idea" about their character or scene idea in their head. The problem is, their fellow players likely have absolutely no idea what's brewing in their eager fellow player's mind and therefore have no idea how to react. No matter how brilliant an idea might be, it's worthless if the entire scene goes bad. The same holds true in meetings – if everyone is caught up "in their own stuff" and not seeing the full picture, the final result will not be as successful.

By using the principles of improv outlined in *The Improv Edge,* teams will quickly experience a sense of pride from all members participating and developing a fun narrative together. Improv techniques assist team members in discovering unique answers to challenges they may be facing. Improv principles promote creative thinking and greatly assist in silencing our inner critics.

There's seldom a plan in improv. Since everything is happening live on stage in front of an audience, there are no do-overs. Scenes cannot be stopped in the middle due to someone saying, "the wrong thing." Improv players must pay attention and respond to things the instant they happen! *There are no leaders.*

Improv principles used by team members are very similar. Old school thinking proposes that an effective team leader must know everything and communicate to everyone what they must do. However, the new team leader looks to the future, is innovative, and deeply knows that their job is to ask the right questions while providing their team with nominal structure and true independence. If someone makes a mistake, everyone needs to jump in and take care of it. Noble work gets accomplished when everyone has each other's back and looks out for the best interest of their teammates.

However, there *are* responsibilities. Everyone must bring their best work to the team. The team cannot be responsible for fixing the mistakes of someone who doesn't bring their A-game. The improviser's mantra of "I got your back" is a bold reminder that trust is present with all team members.

Effective leaders have enormous advantages when they listen and engage in open dialogue with their staff or team members. We cannot attain alignment, empowerment or accountability without enthusiastically engaging our staff. Leaders must be open and accepting, even if they initially disagree. This is where the "yes, and..." improv rules come into play.

In business, most tend to nurture the default response of "yes, *but..."* instead of "yes, *and..."* In doing so, they reject, contradict or in the worst case, ignore their partner's offer. In improv training, we refer to the "yes, but" response as a *denial in a tuxedo.*

This "yes, but..." response first appears to be supportive but takes an undesirable shift when the recipient of the message is advised their input is rejected. To truly communicate, *connection* is required. We must let go of our initial opinion and really engage with what others are bringing to the table. There are four primary steps to shift off our buts...

Magnify your awareness. Accept as many suggestions, offers and propositions as possible. Be in the presence of mind to actively listen. Peek beyond the words spoken and identify the emotions, values, and deeper interests that exist. Effective leadership requires attentiveness.

Say "yes" to what's offered. Simply accept what others are contributing. Remember that doing so doesn't mean you fully agree with what they have provided; it simply means accepting it - without avoiding, ignoring, dismissing or invalidating it. *This requires setting your ego and agenda aside.*

Paraphrase what you've heard. Before moving on, summarize what you've heard and be sure your team members are satisfied that you understood their contribution.

Add to what's emerging. Consider how you can build on the information offered. Perhaps ask a question to identify more details about their vision and add additional details to their offer. This is not meant to be considered a debate of competing ideas, but, as we do in improv, continue in building the story.

Using the rule of "yes, and" as a leadership philosophy does take some courage, but it challenges you to engage your employees, uncover what they are thinking and build from there. Begin approaching every conversation and team meeting interaction as an opportunity to improvise! By doing so, you and your team will cover more ground while experiencing a greater degree of cooperation and imagination!

Your Take-Aways:

- *A successful team requires harmony and cohesion between the team members.*

- *Improv will provide your team with creativity, collaboration and co-creation.*

- *Improv will assist in uncovering new opportunities while letting go of what isn't working.*

- *A successful team requires harmony and cohesion between the team members.*

- *Magnify your awareness, say 'yes' to what's offered, paraphrase what you've heard and add to what is emerging.*

- *Approach every conversation as an opportunity to improvise!*

Chapter 25

Some Final Words from the Author

Okay, so now you've uncovered the fascinating world of improv. Pretty cool, right? And you've also discovered how to plug many of its principles into your work, relationships and life. The key now is to *do it*. Many times, we're educated on a subject but fail to implement it into our day to day lives. Let's delve a bit deeper into the rules of improv and how they can powerfully assist you. Whether on an improv stage, job interview, movie audition, team assembly, staff meeting or handling a disgruntled client or employee, the fascinating world of improv will assist you in many conditions you will encounter!

Appreciate Your Unscripted Life

For the Improv Student: As a student of improv, you're already experiencing the power of it in your everyday life. Begin to recognize the value of spontaneity in your daily interactions. Exercise a playful mind, embrace active listening principles, open collaborating, and creativity. Improv can be scary and rewarding at the same time. Work together to create relationships, environments, situations, and conflicts – all without the comfort of an unnecessary script!

For Everyone Else: As you've hopefully surmised from this book, our life is improvised. The best things in life are experienced when you let yourself go and have fun; that's why we have vacations! The magic happens when we let go of too much structure and allow ourselves space to play. Sure, curveballs will be thrown your way. Expect them, but don't allow them to bog you down. Find joy in saying YES daily!

Practice "Yes, and...!"

For the Improv Student: I'm preaching to the choir on this one. You are already aware of the power of the Rule of Acceptance, right? Agree and add to the message. The only thing I recommend to better utilize the "yes and.." rule is to avoid sounding robotic by other forms of agreement, such as, *"You bet..." "You're right..." "Of course..." "Good idea..."*

For Everyone Else: When meeting with a client, sharing ideas in a team meeting or having a conversation with a friend or partner, *intensely listen to everything*. The "yes, and..." rule is a powerful remedy to workplace negativity. Once all agree to follow, communication is improved through the reduction of barriers, and acceptance is increased. Once you begin your acceptance journey in meeting situations with an energetic "yes," you will transform the way people perceive you!

Don't Block

For the Improv Student: Saying no is the ego's way of attempting to control the future. Don't try to control the future;

make an effort to accept it. The Rule of Acceptance declares that no matter what happens on stage during a scene, you must accept it as real. You don't have to like or believe it, but it's your obligation as a team member to *accept* it. It's not about where we think the scene *should* go but allowing it to go *where it's going*. Saying yes and following through with added information to move the scene forward prevents us from blocking.

For Everyone Else: Life seldom carries itself out exactly as we desire. While we have every right to attempt to alter it, we cannot deny what it brings forth. We must accept whatever is happening at a given time. Whether managing your family, dealing with staff members, contributing to your team's efforts in resolving a challenge put before you or whenever something happens in our lives, which we do not (or cannot) control, we must accept it. Don't be the person who finds "no" a standard response.

Just as in improv, observe how you speak to yourself. Be positive and inspiring. Those who find "Yes" to be a more suitable response are rewarded by adventures. Those who say "No" merely remain with the safety they were already experiencing.

Be Committed, Not Controlling

For the Improv Student: When it comes to improv scenes, you must be fully committed. Nothing is more awkward than watching a scene where participants aren't "all in." One must remain present in an improv scene. You must forget about preparing what you want to say or thinking of a funny line; instead, just allow it to unfold as it comes to you.

For Everyone Else: Life is the same way; the more we attempt to control the outcome, the more difficult it seems to become. When we are present in the moment is when the magic happens, so...

Stay in the Moment

For the Improv Student: If you are obsessing over the past or fretting about the future, you're not going to be present in the scene. An effective improviser must be cognizant of everything on stage. Avoid jumping to where you desire the scene to go. Avoid second-guessing your actions. Pause when necessary to make your contribution to the scene more valuable.

For Everyone Else: Be present. Practice mindfulness (See Chapter 7). Our inner voices are always bantering commentaries based on our experiences. Our inner voice can interrupt our being present in the moment with statements like, *"I wish he would stop talking." "I know what she's going to say next." "I've heard this all before,"* etc.

Wouldn't you like to be recognized as more empathetic? Approachable? Avoid planning the next thing you are going to say. Instead, just actively listen to the person you are having a conversation with. Doing so will take you out of your head. To truly engage other human beings and create meaningful connections, you must silence your inner voices and be fully present. Be mindful and practice mindfulness.

Trust Your Imagination

For the Improv Student: Trust your mind. In an improv scene, we have no time to "think up" a response. There are no wrong answers or cruel gifts for the enlightened improviser. Allow yourself to be surprised and gracefully accept what is put before you because beyond acceptance is appreciation and gratitude.

For Everyone Else: In life, the more we use our instincts and intuition, the stronger they become. Most successful people attribute the tool of "gut instincts" to their success.

Practice Mutual Support

For the Improv Student: It is necessary to support your fellow players and allow them to support you. In everyday life, we often desire to do everything alone. We have a vision of the result, and we want it done the way we envision it. With improv, we must learn to rely on and support others. Bonding works.

For Everyone Else: Look into the eyes of your partner, spouse or co-worker for 30 seconds straight. Difficult? Weird? Sure, it may seem intense, but it's a fabulous bonding exercise. Bonding makes a give-and-take dialog easier to accomplish.

Minimize Questions

For the Improv Student: Questions are a no-no in improv. If you are asking a question, then you're likely not contributing to the conversation. Questions have an empty value in an improv scene. They are a lazy way out, placing the burden of creativity on your scene partner to fill in the information. That's not fair. In improv, every detail is a choice. If you avoid committing to a choice, decision, or detail, you are not doing your part, and the scene will indeed suffer. Like most improv rules, there are exceptions. Good questions that energetically move the conversation forward are okay.

For Everyone Else: The idea of avoiding questions can readily apply to the workplace and life as well. You are not expected to know everything, but the next time you feel the desire to ask a question of a supervisor or colleague, why not offer a proactive solution to the question you are about to ask? In doing so, you are being proactive. You become a thoughtful, resourceful contributor to the conversation.

Instead of saying, *"Are we planning to bring this concept to our existing clients?"* Try a more proactive approach instead, *"I think this would be a great concept to bring to our existing clients"*

Listen

For the Improv Student: Practice active listening during improv scenes. Refine your abilities to focus and engage completely with your fellow players. Seek to recognize and understand their message, cues and body language while comprehending the verbal information.

For Everyone Else: I'm sure you've heard about "those people" who speak but aren't talking about anything, right? Improv is all about thoughtful, pertinent contribution to detail because it's what keeps your scene partner and the audience engaged. Before speaking, ask yourself these questions:

> *"What is my objective by saying this?"*
> *"What do I desire to accomplish?"*

These questions will not only tighten your focus on the subject at hand but also ensure that what you're about to say has value. Incessantly speaking without demonstrating an authentic contribution to a conversation is a guaranteed solution to being ignored.

Recognize Mistakes as Gifts

For the Improv Student: You're not going to be a happy camper when your mistake screwed up a scene. Don't fret, though. We've all done it and will continue to do it; just learn from it. The mere fact you are more cognizant of errors are the building blocks to being a better performer. Improv teaches us that there is a reason for everything. Find the gem contained in the blunder, pull it out, brush it off and discover the gem contained within it!

For Everyone Else: Admitting we made a mistake is the first step to growing and improving in our life, relationship or business. Acknowledge the bungle and reflect on what can be done differently next time to avoid it from happening again. If you're afraid of making a mistake, you are more likely to restrain your creative ideas.

In order to share creative ideas, everyone needs to feel safe. People will not share their ideas if they don't feel safe and fear feeling or looking foolish. Make people feel safe. Successful people don't see failures; they see them as experiments. They translate them into learning opportunities. Mistakes become gifts when we learn from them!

Embrace the Fear

For the Improv Student: Fear is a common thing for new improv students. However, they soon discover that embracing it will many times lead to some amazing moments! Getting unwrapped from our comfy zones places us in a new dimension of creativity. As a progressive improviser, go all in on a scene or character choice!

For Everyone Else: We become wrapped up in our comforts. From our favorite foods to the route we take to the office, we have become victims of life's comfortable processes. Fear often manifests itself when there's something we know we desire, but we're hesitant to try it because we feel we may be rejected, fail or just disappointed with the experience. When this happens, respond to it with *action*. Step off the beaten path in your life. Try new things. New experiences force us to grow!

I highly recommend you go back through *The Improv Edge*, this time focusing on the chapters where more "work" is needed. There's a difference between knowing something and practicing it. Book knowledge is only valuable to those who practice and put it to work in their lives.

We talked about *Neuroplasticity* - the ability of the brain to physically change structure and operation based on stimuli, behaviors and thoughts. By practicing the principles in *The Improv Edge*, you will begin making new neuronal connections in your brain. Neuroplasticity is like a superpower that we all can develop to change ourselves and close the gap between knowing and doing. By consciously acting with mindful intent, the "work" is well worth it!

Okay, it's time to get to work, my friend!

IMPROV...A CURE FOR CONTROL FREAKS

Once upon a time, there was a middle-aged woman who loved to create entertaining videos and speak to live audiences. This woman loved starring and presenting in videos because she would be completely prepared. She would rehearse exactly what she was going to say in the videos and had trusty PowerPoint slides to keep her on track when speaking to her audience. The certainty of it all was very comforting to her.

The more prepared she was, the more confident she felt. If she made a mistake while talking in the video, no problem, she would either edit the mistake out or, even better, re-shoot the video until she liked every word.

Yes, you could say this woman liked to feel "in control." Perhaps this could be blamed on her five-foot stature of not feeling tall enough. She had a wacky notion that if she couldn't be powerful in height, she could be powerful in preparation and presentations."

Everything was going great until she tried improv...

Wait a minute! You mean to tell me, I can't prepare? I can't have a head's up on what my stage partner is going to say or do? Do I have to just be free in my thinking? Do I have to be present and not allow my mind to race ahead of the scene? Do I have to trust myself and, most of all, the person I'm improvising with? And the whole premise of improv is to have someone else's back and not just think of myself?

To make them a superstar, and all will be good in the hood?

And that's when the little woman fell over and realized... there's more to life than just herself. What an ah-ha moment that was.

That short woman was me, and I'm proud to say, I've grown. Well, not vertically but emotionally. Thru improv, I learned that letting go of control and predicting how things are going to turn out was probably the best tough love I could give myself.

I'm not going to sugar coat it and say I enjoyed acting out the Battle of Anzio (which I knew nothing about) or that I relished in the spontaneity of a scene where I was a certified pork inspector. You see, it doesn't really matter if you know anything about the topic; what matters is that you are willing to admit you don't know... and that's okay. Sometimes, the most beautiful and entertaining scenes are the ones where people have no clue what they are talking about. All that matters is that they are listening to each other and have each other's back.

Just imagine, if everyone in the world adopted that rule of improv.

If you find yourself always needing to be prepared and in control, you should talk to your doctor about improv. But note, possible side effects from taking improv are freedom, improved listening skills, laughing, crying, laughing until you're crying, laughing leakage, irritable laughing and the inability to stop laughing!

Jenny Weldon
CreativeMessageMedia.com
Scottsdale, Arizona

I'm a computer scientist and mathematician. Three years ago, in the spur of the moment, I took an improv workshop. It was love at first sight and I have been doing improv ever since (both short form and long form).

It has given me the confidence to explore other artistic expressions such as acting, playwriting, screenwriting, and even standup!

All of these pursuits have enriched my life in ways I could have never imagined, and it all began with saying 'YES AND' to Improv!

Karthik C. S.
Postdoctoral Researcher, New York University
New York City, New York

Chapter 26

Improv in the Movies

Hollywood directors recognize and embrace the benefits of improv as well. There are many scenes where the spontaneity of the actors has given them the courage to go off-script and improvise a line during a scene. Many have gone on to become classic, highly recalled passages in the movies.

Some of the best comedy actors in the world have their roots in improvisation, Melissa McCarthy, Ryan Reynolds, Tina Fey, Amy Poehler and Julia Louis-Dreyfus, to name a few.

> *Some of the best comedy actors in the world have their roots in improvisation*

Steve Carell's creative cursing during his chest waxing scene in *The 40-Year-Old Virgin*. Every swear word was improvised in direct response to the real pain he was experiencing.

Sacha Baron Cohen's many scenes in *Borat* as well as *This is Spinal Tap* included dozens of improvised scenes.

There were many improvised lines in *Jaws*, including the iconic, *"You're gonna need a bigger boat"* statement uttered by actor Roy Schneider.

Jack Nicholson's classic line, *"Here's Johnny"* in *The Shining* was improvised. Nicholson said it was borrowed from Ed McMahon's nightly introduction of Johnny Carson on *The Tonight Show.*

In *The Godfather*, Director Francis Ford Coppola's script called for the line, *"Leave the gun."* When it came time to film the scene, actor Richard Castellano, playing mobster Clemenza, improvised by adding... *"take the cannoli."*

In *Bridesmaids*, Maya Rudolph's character takes a dump in the middle of the street in a wedding dress after coming down with food poisoning. It wasn't in the script but became a classic scene in the movie.

In *A Few Good Men*, Jack Nicholson's line, *"You can't handle the truth"* was his own improvised version from the original screenplay line, *"You already have the truth."*

Humphrey Bogart's famous line in *Casablanca*, *"Here's looking at you, kid"* was first uttered off camera while he was teaching Ingrid Bergman how to play poker between takes. It later came out spontaneously during one of the Paris flashback scenes and became an all-time classic line of the movie.

Marty Feldman articulated the humorous line, *"What hump?"* as Igor in *Young Frankenstein*. That improvised remark was worked into the script because of his occasionally shifting the hump on his back as a physical prank to get a laugh from the other cast members.

In *Goodfellas,* Director Martin Scorsese gave Joe Pesci and Ray Liotta the go-ahead to improvise a restaurant scene. The lines, *"What do you mean funny? Funny how? Funny like I'm a clown, I amuse you?"* were based on dialogue from an encounter Pesci had with an actual mobster years earlier at a restaurant where he was employed. The other actors in the scene had no idea what was coming.

In *Animal House,* John Belushi's famous *"I'm a zit, get it?"* cafeteria scene was fully improvised.

In *Teenage Mutant Ninja Turtles* – the actors who played the computer-generated turtle characters, were goofing around and freestyling rap between takes. The director liked their improvisational work and asked them to do it on camera. It was then converted into an improvised CG masterpiece.

Peter Farrelly, one of the directors of *Dumb and Dumber,* said that 15% of their film was improvised.

Will Ferrell, in *Anchorman: The Legend of Ron Burgundy,* had so many improvised scenes that they made a whole other film out of the offshoots.

There are many more instances where actors have drawn upon their talents of improvisation in their on-screen personas. *Improv can assist you too!*

I am a professional clothier in New York City. In an average day I make over 80 cold calls to build relationships with C-level executives throughout the city. I face many objections and it's very time consuming and tedious.

After attending my first improv class I learned a different approach, and that is to accept situations as they are and to adjust to them, opposed to trying to adjust the situation itself. I also found that using statements instead of questions creates a better flow of dialogue.

To me, improv will sharpen my sales techniques to be consistent and open up more opportunities for conversation. I'll use these skills in overcoming objections as well as working with clients to create a clearer line of communication. I have no doubt that continuing improv will grow my sales!

Andrew Carrillo
Professional Clothier
New York City, New York

Chapter 27

Let the Games Begin

Okay, so now you're aware of the many powerful components of improvisation and how they can positively influence your life, organization, relationships or career.

That known, this book wouldn't be complete without a few improv exercises to assist in the techniques discussed throughout the chapters.

Let's have some fun and look at a few short-form improv games that'll assist in sharpening your *IMPROVabilities!*

They're easy to do, just assemble a few friends, co-workers or team members and give em a go!

Improvisers Hannah Heard and Joe Hammer...
obviously saddened about *something!*

Photo courtesy of Elizabeth George Photography

Yes, and...

Aim: Listening, Collaboration and Teamwork

Players: 2

Time: 2 minutes or less

This is not only a game, but as you know, it's a fundamental rule of improv, *the Rule of Agreement!* The premise is quite simple; a dialog is started between two players. After hearing the declaration from your fellow player, you must respond in the affirmative while adding supporting information. Avoid, "yes, *but...*"

This process is "ping-ponged" back and forth between players. Refer to Chapter #15, for a more detailed explanation of this celebrated improv directive.

Player #1: *I can't wait to go sky diving tomorrow!*

Player #2: *Yes, and I'm sure your parachute will be safely packed!*

Player #1: *Yes, and I trust my instructor do a good job.*

Player #2: *Yes, and if he doesn't, you won't have to worry about trying it again!*

You can also use other affirmative connectors, such as *"Sure..." "Okay..." "Of course..."* etc., but it's best to get accustomed to using *"Yes, and..."* until you're comfortable with the agreement process.

The Blank Page

Aim: Creativity and Storytelling
Players: Solo scene to audience or team
Time: 3 minutes or less

You show a blank piece of paper. Your task
is to explain what's "on" it by referencing it
as a photograph of a real or imagined event in your life. You
address many elements and details of the photo.

> *"This is a photo of my family vacation when I was*
> *a kid. I think I was 10."*
>
> *"That's me and that's my sister, Marsha."*
>
> *"I loved that beach. We went parasailing."*
>
> *"That's my little friend, Doug."*

Be sure to make eye contact with others as you explain the
details. Connect.

> *"That's my brother, Mike. I miss him so much. I*
> *remember his dog; he was a funny looking little thing.*
> *His name was Scruffy."*

Conclude by thanking the audience for allowing you to share
your precious memories!

Emotional Gibberish

Aim: Right brain thinking and acting

Players: Two

Time: 2 minutes or less

This is a game of creativity and emotion development. This exercise allows us to dismiss our standard language response and, instead, respond to the *emotions* behind the "words."

It is a conversation where one player speaks in gibberish, using various emotions, while the other players responds as though they understand.

For example, I could look sad, drop my head, frown and say, *"Mamoosh ala kinsa boyshun."*

My partner could respond with, *"Oh, Joe... I'm so sorry to hear that your pet hamster died."*

The dialog continues with different facial expressions and body movement, thus offering more diverse reactions. After the response, I can then perk up and say, *"Bow-sha butta see-wa, carta sayla!"*

Seeing the change in my demeane, my partner responds with, *"Well, that's nice that your Chihuahua is still alive, though!"*

Borrowed Banter

Aim: Listening

Players: 2 or more

Time: 2 minutes or less

Two players engage in dialog where they use a word (or words) from their fellow player's previous sentence.

Player #1:

"Hey Mike, I love your new backpack; it looks like it has a lot of **space**."

Player #2:

"I gotta tell ya Mike, I don't think I'm going to have enough **space** in my new apartment."

Player #1:

"Did you hear we may be **sending** a man to Mars? I love **space** exploration."

Player #2:

"I was talking to Jimmy, and he said he was **sending** his kid away to **boarding** school.

Player #1:

"My son is entering a skate**boarding** competition in the city on Friday.

Emotional Transfer

Aim: Listening and Acting

Players: 2

Time: 2 minutes or less

Two players engage in dialog where they each start with one emotion and slowly during the dialog, change the emotion, transferring it over to their fellow player, who does the same thing.

Fun and easily demonstrable emotions could include:

Afraid	*Enthused*	*Restless*	*Jealous*	*Nostalgic*
Agitated	*Excited*	*Serene*	*Impatient*	*Nervous*
Lonely	*Feisty*	*Skeptical*	*Confused*	*Detached*
Angry	*Frightened*	*Uptight*	*Hyper*	*Mischievous*
Clueless	*Proud*	*Nervous*	*Bored*	*Disappointed*

Unqualified Expert

Aim: Acting and Spontaneity

Players: 2 or more

Time: 3 minutes or less

Players engage in dialog where one is an expert in any given field – real or made-up.

Other players interview and ask questions of this expert.

The expert then articulates unusual answers relating to their expertise.

Use your imagination!

First Line Last Line

Aim: Listening and Collaboration

Players: 2

Time: 2 minutes or less

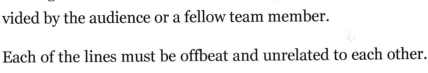

Players engage in a brief scene with dialog, starting with the first line and last lines provided by the audience or a fellow team member.

Each of the lines must be offbeat and unrelated to each other. For example:

First line:

"I enjoy walking my lizard during Arizona rainstorms."

Last line:

"My aunt can levitate after holding her breath for a few minutes."

During the conversation, each member must be aware of the last line and gently segue towards it while keeping the dialong sounding like a natural conversation.

Questions Only

Aim: Listening and Right Brain Thinking

Players: 2

Time: 3 minutes or less

In improv, we don't ask questions, but this game allows it! Players engage in a scene but cannot make statements; they can only converse in questions.

Further, they cannot parrot back a question already asked. For example, a parroted response to *"Hey, would you like to go to the park?"* could be, *"Have you ever been to the park?"*

> **Player #1:** *Would you like to go to the dance with me tonight?*
> **Player #2:** *What should I wear?*
> **Player #1:** *Can you do the hokey-pokey?*
> **Player #2:** *Have you ever put your left foot in?*
> **Player #1:** *Are those your dancing shoes?*
> **Player #2:** *What time do you have to be home?*

Continue the dialog as quickly as possible, keeping the dialog moving until a player incorrectly utters a statement instead of a question.

One Word Story

Aim: Listening, Spontaneity and Teamwork

Players: 2 - 20

Time: 3 minutes or less

Two or more players engage in a story by each adding one word at a time. The topic can be chosen by an audience member or fellow team member. Each player takes a turn, speaking only one word per turn. Avoid interjecting weird or non-applicable words that don't resonate with the story.

Avoid using "and" too many times.

Player #1: *My*

Player #2: *Dad*

Player #3: *Said*

Player #4: *My*

Player #5: *Mom*

Player #1: *Is*

Player #2: *Afraid*

Player #3: *Of*

Player #4: *Small*

Player #5: *Lizards*

Players must be cognizant and stop when the story reaches a logical conclusion.

Facetime

Aim: Creativity and Acting

Players: 2 or more

Time: 2 minutes or less

Facetime is a zany game where players are assigned an emotion and must demonstrate it by making a face that best reflects the emotion during a given scene.

The player must maintain the face during the entire scene, as if they were wearing a mask.

Play "big" on your visual characteristics and stay in character with the assigned emotion.

Easily demonstrable facial emotions could include:

Afraid	*Enthused*	*Restless*	*Jealous*	*Nostalgic*
Agitated	*Excited*	*Serene*	*Impatient*	*Nervous*
Lonely	*Feisty*	*Skeptical*	*Confused*	*Detached*
Angry	*Frightened*	*Uptight*	*Hyper*	*Mischievous*
Clueless	*Proud*	*Nervous*	*Bored*	*Disappointed*

Magazine Mayhem

Aim: Creativity and Listening

Players: 3

Time: 3 minutes or less

Two players are given two different magazines. The magazines are to be referenced for spoken lines by these two players during the scene.

A topic is suggested by the audience or team member.

The third player's job is to stand between the two players with magazines and make up dialog related to the scene, while responding to the statements made by the two players who are reciting random lines from the magazines. They must [attempt to] connect and make sense of the lines delivered by their fellow players.

Don't "look for" applicable lines that may fit the scene. Just flip to a page, scan and read a random line. Don't read too many lines; just a line or two is enough.

Another version of this game can be done using text messages from an audience members' or teammates' cell phones, but this can get weird, so fasten your seatbelts if you choose to try it!

Superheroes

Aim: Creativity and Teamwork

Players: 3 - 5

Time: 5 minutes or less

Player one solicits an imaginary world-threatening crisis from a team or audience member. They also ask for a superpower and superhero name for each of the remaining players. The name must be unusual or obscure and reflect the superhero's powers, such as *Boneless Boy, Super Glue Man, Smelly Garlic Girl* or *Captain Coach Potato.*

Player one calls out for assistance from the first superhero. The called upon superhero enters the scene, explaining in a few sentences how they will use their assigned superhero powers to assist in conquering the crisis.

They conclude by calling in another superhero by referencing their assigned name.

Each of the Superheroes call upon their colleague until all of the superheroes have entered the scene, with the last one explaining how they have all been successful in overcoming and resolving the world crisis!

Sorry I'm Late

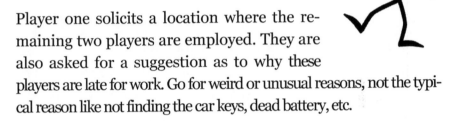

Aim: Creativity and Teamwork

Players: 3

Time: 4 minutes or less

Player one solicits a location where the remaining two players are employed. They are also asked for a suggestion as to why these players are late for work. Go for weird or unusual reasons, not the typical reason like not finding the car keys, dead battery, etc.

Player two accepts this excuse, while Player three's job is to reinforce and justify their fellow employee's excuse while it is being explained to the supervisor. It is their job to add supporting dialog, bringing life to the excuse. Player one then sets the scene as a supervisor in his office, when the two players enter the scene – late to work. The supervisor asks why they're so late, and the zany scene begins!

Player #1: *You're late...*

Player #2: *I know... I was chased away from my car by an alligator this morning.*

Player #3: *Yes, I really thought he was going to be eaten alive!*

Player #1: *An alligator...*

Player #2: *Yes, it was mad because of the crocodile logo embroidered on my shirt.*

Player #3: *Yes, alligators can grow up to 15 feet; this one was almost 14.*

Player #1: *Interesting that you were able to measure it...*

A Bunch of Blanks

Aim: Creativity and Fast Thinking
Players: 3 or more
Time: 5 minutes or less

This is an atypical "bar joke" where the audience provides suggestions for a number of common occupations, professions, animals or the like. Players then step forward and recite the joke, ending with a punchline as it relates to the chosen suggestions. The dialog is as follows:

> *A bunch of_____ walk into the bar and the bartender said, "I'll be with you in a minute," and the _____s replied, "[related punchline]"*

For example,

Deaf cheerleaders. A bunch of deaf cheerleaders walk into the bar, and the bartender said, "I'll be with you in a minute," and the deaf cheerleaders replied, *"What?"* [while jumping to a cheer]

Psychics. A bunch of psychics walk into the bar, and the bartender said, "I'll be with you in a minute," and the psychics replied, *"Duh, we already knew that!"*

Attorneys. A bunch of attorneys walk into the bar, and the bartender said "I'll be with you in a minute," and the attorneys replied, *"Forget it, we'll just pass this bar."*

Alphabet Story

Aim: Listening and Storytelling

Players: 2

Time: 4 minutes or less

Two players engage in a scene's dialog. The first player begins their sentence with a word, starting with the letter "A." The next player must respond and continue the conversation with their sentence beginning with the letter "B." This continues back and forth until the entire alphabet is used.

Player #1: *Alright Tommy, here you go – the keys to your new car!*

Player #2: *Boy dad, I never thought I'd get a corvette for my first car.*

Player #1: *Compare that to the neighbor kid's junky Hyundai!*

Player #2: *Don't think I could ever be seen in THAT at my school.*

Player #1: *Everyone would probably laugh at you.*

Player #2: *For real, although Cindy has a Porsche.*

Player #1: *Gosh, I'm sorry I can't afford a Porsche for you Tommy.*

Player #2: *Hug me, Dad; you're still the best!*

Evil Twins

Aim: Listening and Teamwork

Players: 4

Time: 4 minutes or less

Two players begin dialog in a scene. The other two players are the first two player's "evil twins."

At any point during the dialog, the "twins" can yell *freeze!,* tag out their twin and continue the scene but taking it in a malevolent and malicious direction.

After doing so, they step away from the scene.

The original twin brother then steps back in and proceeds to justify and explain the evil, attempting to rationalize and correct the damage that was done by the evil twin while continuing the scene.

Verses

Aim: Listening and Fast Thinking

Players: 2 or more

Time: 3 minutes or less

Two players exchange dialog but do so in verses. The first player offers the first line of dialog, with the second player rhyming to it. Then the second player offers a second non-rhyming line, and the first player responds with a statement rhyming with that. Any players who hesitates or fails to rhyme are lovingly sent off stage and replaced by other players.

Player #1: *I think I'm going to my girl's house for a fine dinner <u>tonight</u>!*

Player #2: *That's nice; be careful not to get into a <u>fight</u>! Her kids may be joining you both for dinner as <u>well</u>.*

Player #1: *I hope not, last time it wasn't all that <u>swell</u>. They almost choked on her macaroni and <u>cheese</u>.*

Player #2: *That never happens to me... I always swallow it with <u>ease</u>. I bet she's going to be excited to see <u>you</u>...*

Player #1: *Yes she will... like the morning grass embraces the sunrise <u>dew</u>. You should get a girlfriend; they make life <u>fun</u>...*

Player #2: *I did, but after two weeks I was totally <u>done</u>.*

Definition Rendition

Aim: Storytelling

Players: Solo scene to audience or team

Time: 3 minutes or less

The audience or fellow team member provides a made-up, nonsensical word. The player's job is to explain the word's definition, perhaps its origin, concluding by using it in a sentence.

Audience suggestion: *Pelicadormatoriam*

Pelicadormatoriam... the Pelicadormatoriam is a little-known building south of the Mediterranean sea where full-grown North African pelicans seek temporary shelter. This is normally done during the fish school year, and...

Lines from a Hat

Aim: Storytelling

Players: 2

Time: 3 minutes or less

Audience or fellow team members write a number of random sentences and statements on small slips of paper. No questions. The weirder the better... *"I can lift a 300-pound pig over my head." "My dog likes pickles." "I know a guy who licks his shoes." "My uncle is allergic to his reflection."*

These lines are collected and placed into a hat. Two players take the stage, each reaching into the hat and taking out three of the lines, placing them into their pocket without looking at them.

The audience or fellow team members now give a suggestion for the scene. The players begin dialog relating to the scene. At some point during the dialog, they have to pull out one of the slips of paper, read what's on it, say the line and integrate it into the scene.

The scene then continues with each player doing so until all slips are read, and the scene is brought to a logical conclusion.

Headlines

Aim: Listening and Concentration

Players: 2 or more

Time: N/A

In this exercise, players come up with out-landish headlines. The twist is that the last word of a player's headline becomes the first word of the next player's headline. This a great exercise for warming up and can include all members of the group or team.

Player #1: *Gorilla chases maintenance employee out of the Phoenix zoo.*

Player #2: *Zoo closes due to shortage of cages for the animals.*

Player #3: *Animals have been proven to be smarter than adults.*

Player #4: *Adults have been banned from Starbucks.*

Player #5: *Starbucks releases new biscuits and gravy flavored coffee.*

Player #6: *Coffee found to contain traces of unknown substance from Mars.*

About the Author

Since being exposed to *The Upright Citizens Brigade* in New York City decades ago, Joe Hammer has studied and embraced the principles of improvisation in his life, career and training programs. As a business development speaker, author and entertainer, Joe has provided many training programs to progressive organizations, companies and entrepreneurs. His passion for improvisation and entertaining is always part of the mix in his programs.

Joe has assisted clients in banishing life-long challenges, limitations and habits through his *Rapid Changeworks* hypnotherapy practice, some of which are referenced in his book, *The Unconscious Authority*.

On the fun side, Joe has entertained audiences with his unique Magic-Comedy and Stage Hypnosis shows, as well as performing and teaching Improvisation Comedy. Improv training has skyrocketed in popularity, and progressive businesses have increasingly turned to Joe for help with their company's team building and communication efficiency training needs.

Co-creation, spontaneity and clarity are benchmarks in all of Joe's training programs. It's not uncommon for him to appear on corporate offsites or hold specialized group improv training for progressive organizations.

Joe conducts training classes for both new and seasoned students who have an interest in improvisation theater. He also heads up the improv troupe, *The Outcasters,* based in Scottsdale, Arizona.

If you'd like to bring Joe's improv training into your organization, learn improv or even join *The Outcasters* for a show or class, please visit:

www.TheOutcasters.com
www.YourImprovCoach.com
Virtual and live classes are available

For more information on Joe's business development programs, mentoring and consulting services, please visit:

www.ThatSmallBusinessGuy.com

For more information on Joe's book, *The Unconscious Authority: How to Break Through Your Mind's Barriers, Unleash Your Dormant Wisdom and Banish Limitations in Your Life, Relationships or Career,* please visit:

www.UnconsciousAuthority.com

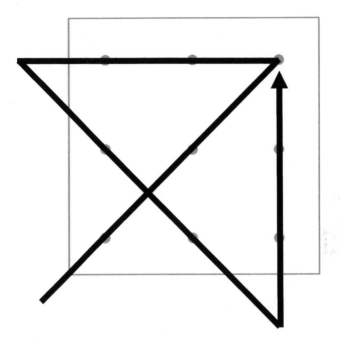

The nine dot puzzle represents the time-worn phrase, *"Think outside the box,"* however its message is quite clear:

> *We confine ourselves to thinking within our preconceived notions and historic programming*

This programming relates to what we *believe* to be the "rules" in that the puzzle appears difficult because we assume we must stay within the boundary around the dot array, *even though it is not mentioned in the instructions.*

This is a *perceived barrier.* The lessons in improv reflect the solution to this puzzle:

> *Step away from historic programming and open up your mind to a new world of solutions!*